Unlocking the Seer Gift

by Regina Shank

Copyright

The Seer Gift

By Regina Shank

Copyright © 2021

All rights reserved. This book is protected by the copyright laws of the United States of America. This book may not be copied or reprinted for commercial gain or profit. The use of short quotations or occasional page copying for personal or group study is encouraged. Permission will be granted upon request from Regina Shank. Unless otherwise stated, all biblical quotations are taken from the New International Version (NIV). All rights reserved. Any emphasis added to Scripture quotations is the author's own.

Editing/Layout by Jim Bryson
(JamesLBryson@gmail.com)

Graphics by David Munoz
(DavidMunoznvtn@gmail.com)

Table of Contents

Notes to the Reader v

Definitions xv

Foreword 1

1. The Spirit Realm 5

2. Dreams and Visions 15

3. Purity of Heart 25

4. Perspective 31

5. Misconceptions Debunked 39

6. What Will Be, Will Be? 49

7. The Power of Courage 65

8. The Kingdom 73

9. Ascendancy of the Spirit 83

10. Servant or Son? 91

About the Author 103

Notes to the Reader

UNLOCKING THE SEER REALM is purposed to unlock the ability to see spiritually with the eyes of the heart. There are keys to unlock this ability that are inherent within each person. Keys are mentioned throughout this book. I have marked them with a picture of a key, so you can find them easily. I have also boldfaced actual seer experiences that reinforce the text of this book. There are principles on the pages, but also experiences from present-day seers. New Testament basis for the existence of seers today is also unpacked within its pages.

The Old Testament lists several seers; among them is Iddo, King Solomon's seer. His name means "timely" or "his time." He is listed in 2 Chronicles 12:15 and 9:29. He lived during the reigns of King Solomon and his heirs, Rehoboam and Abijah, in the Kingdom of Judah. He must have been a young man when he stepped into the office of official king's seer, because he outlived his boss and served in that office for Solomon's descendants.

David's seer was Gad. He is listed in I Samuel 22:5 where he gave a warning to David when he was running from King Saul. He is also listed in 2 Samuel 24:11-12. Gad worked with the prophet Nathan to bring forth prophetic visions to give wisdom, warning, and knowledge of future happenings.

> He stationed the Levites in the temple of the Lord with cymbals, harps and lyres in the way prescribed by David and Gad the king's seer and Nathan the prophet; this was commanded by the Lord through his prophets.
>
> 2 Chronicles 29:25 NIV

Another Old Testament seer was Heman. His name means, "faithful." He was the grandson of Samuel the prophet and went on to become King David's seer. He had fourteen sons and three daughters. These children were given him through the promises of God to exalt him. He is listed as the King's seer in I Chronicles 25:5.

One notable seer from the New Testament is the Apostle Paul. In this passage (below), Paul does not refer to himself as the one having these experiences, but many scholars believe he was referring to himself.

His statement in 2 Corinthians 12:1-4 gives the impression that Paul is talking about himself:

> *I must go on boasting. Although there is nothing to be gained, I will go on to visions and revelations from the Lord. I know a man in Christ who fourteen years ago was caught up to the third heaven. Whether it was in the body or out of the body I do not know—God knows. And I know that this man—whether in the body or apart from the body I do not know, but God knows— was caught up to paradise and heard inexpressible things, things that no one is permitted to tell.*

Notes to the Reader

Peter also was immensely impacted by his vision on the rooftop in Acts 10:9-16 NIV:

> *About noon the following day as they were on their journey and approaching the city, Peter went up on the roof to pray. He became hungry and wanted something to eat, and while the meal was being prepared, he fell into a trance. He saw heaven opened and something like a large sheet being let down to earth by its four corners. It contained all kinds of four-footed animals, as well as reptiles and birds. Then a voice told him, "Get up, Peter. Kill and eat."*
>
> *"Surely not, Lord!" Peter replied. "I have never eaten anything impure or unclean."*
>
> *The voice spoke to him a second time, "Do not call anything impure that God has made clean."*
>
> *This happened three times, and immediately the sheet was taken back to heaven."*

There are some Christians who would say these seer experiences are not for today. My perspective is the opposite. I have experienced visions, dreams, open visions, and heavenly scenes through the eyes of my heart that have been opened; enlightened by the Spirit of the Lord. I did not grow up in an environment of seers, but through a hungry desperation for the Lord, He opened up my vision to "see" in the realm of the Spirit.

One of the visions I experienced, became the foundation for my second book, *Deliverance to Freedom, A Guide to Releasing Captives*. Retold here:

Years ago, I stepped into a vision of an endless corridor lined with prison cells. Each holding a person. There were no doors on these cells, only solid bars incarcerating the prisoners. As I walked along, gazing into each cell, the Lord said, "I want you to free them."

I said, "There are no doors on these cells. How do I free them?"

His voice resounded, like thunder that shook the prison. "I Am the Door!"

At that moment, doors appeared, opened up, and the way was made for each person to come out of their bondage. I began pulling them out; some refused to come, choosing the "safety" of the familiar place, rather than the liberty they had never known.

Another open vision, that thrust me into my calling to prepare the way of the Lord, I experienced while sitting at a desk in my home office. Suddenly, the Lord invited me into a realm that had not previously been open to me. It was as if He asked me to enter. I could see the open door in my spirit. It was much like Revelation 4:1 where the Lord invited John to come up and see.

> *"After this I looked, and there before me was a door standing open in heaven. And the voice I had first heard speaking to me like a trumpet said, "Come up here, and I will show you what must take place after this."*
>
> Revelation 4:1

Notes to the Reader

The first time He invited me, I did not go into the vision. I was afraid I wouldn't be able to come back to this realm. The Lord was patient with me and invited me a second time. This time I accepted. Suddenly, I was standing in the Jordan River with Jesus and John the Baptist. I knew the Lord wanted to baptize me into this anointing to "prepare the way of the Lord." I was familiar with several scriptures that described this calling.

> *A voice of one calling: "In the wilderness prepare the way for the Lord; make straight in the desert a highway for our God. Every valley shall be raised up, every mountain and hill made low; the rough ground shall become level, the rugged places a plain.*
>
> Isaiah 40:3-4
>
> *"I will send my messenger, who will prepare the way before me. Then suddenly the Lord you are seeking will come to his temple; the messenger of the covenant, whom you desire, will come," says the Lord Almighty.*
>
> Malachi 3:1
>
> *This is he who was spoken of through the prophet Isaiah: "A voice of one calling in the wilderness, 'Prepare the way for the Lord, make straight paths for him.'"*
>
> Matthew 3:3
>
> *"A voice of one calling in the wilderness, 'Prepare the way for the Lord, make straight paths for him.'"*
>
> Mark 1:3

> "And you, my child, will be called a prophet of the Most High; for you will go on before the Lord to prepare the way for him,"
>
> Luke 1:76
>
> As it is written in the book of the words of Isaiah the prophet: "A voice of one calling in the wilderness, 'Prepare the way for the Lord, make straight paths for him.'"
>
> Luke 3:4

John the Baptist had the mantle to prepare the way of the Lord, so in the vison he was there to mantle me with that calling and anointing.

> "In those days John the Baptist came, preaching in the wilderness of Judea and saying, 'Repent, for the kingdom of heaven has come near.' This is he who was spoken of through the prophet Isaiah: "A voice of one calling in the wilderness, 'Prepare the way for the Lord, make straight paths for him.'"
>
> Matthew 3:1-3

I remember standing in the river with Jesus on one side of me and John the Baptist on the other. I was dipped into the river, brought up out of the water, standing in between them, when John the Baptist disappeared. It was then that Jesus and I were at the bottom of a waterfall. I don't recall being wet from the water but was given a blanket of sorts to put on my shoulders. At the bottom of the waterfall, a fire was burning. Jesus and I sat around it. We drank something tasting of fruit, the fluid thick in my mouth. Its substance was somewhere in between liquid and solid.

I was then given a moment to sit with the Lord and warm myself by the fire when an angel came and Jesus left with him. Suddenly, I was in my chair in the home office.

Once I followed Jesus into this new realm, further experiences were opened to me. I sought out biblical basis for them; to substantiate them with others who had had similar experience in the realm of the Spirit. I read Jim Goll's book, *The Seer Realm*. It gave me some peace as to the reality of what I was experiencing. I read about the seers in the Old and New Testaments. I began to hear of others, who had seen spiritual things in the way of visions and dreams. One of the chapters in this book is on the attribute of Courage. It has taken courage for me to write this book. There are many naysayers out there, who have dismissed any opportunity to hear from heaven or experience heaven's input into their lives while on this earth. Those experiences have been relegated to the "sweet by and by" or when we get to heaven.

When I read John 17:3 AMP, I was filled with the courage necessary to write this book. It says:

> *Now this is eternal life: that they may know You, the only true [supreme and sovereign] God, and [in the same manner know] Jesus [as the] Christ whom You have sent."*

Eternal life is not somewhere, sometime. It is knowing Jesus. It begins now…if we are able to open our heart to Him, come into relationship with Him, and conquer our fears of the unknown. I emphasize in this book the importance of closing any open doors from the dark side of spiritual knowledge through repentance prior to entering the spiritual realm by the power of Holy Spirit. But that realm, the fourth dimension, is available to us.

As you read this book, realize that Jesus is relational. Three days after his resurrection, He was on the road to Emmaus. In Luke 24, His experience with Cleopas and his friend was life-changing for them. He did not tell them to read it in a book. He walked with them, talked with them, ate with them, opened the scriptures to them, and caused their hearts to burn within them as they walked that road with Him.

Yes, I read the Bible. I love the Word of God. In John 1, we read that the "Word became flesh and dwelt among us." The Word is relational. Yes, it is historical, but also living, and active, sharper than a two-edged sword. According to Hebrews 4:12 AMP:

> *For the word of God is living and active and full of power [making it operative, energizing, and effective]. It is sharper than any two-edged sword, penetrating as far as the division of the soul and spirit [the completeness of a person], and of both joints and marrow [the deepest parts of our nature], exposing and judging the very thoughts and intentions of the heart.*

History books can't reach the deepest parts of our nature, nor have the ability to expose and judge the very thoughts and intents of our hearts. The Word is living. I will never forget the times the Word seemed to jump off the page at me, providing answers I had just prayed about. You think Google is listening and reading your Facebook page, and monitoring your interests, so they can sell you something? God is greater, omnipresent, omniscient, and greatly interested in your life, your calling, and your concerns.

This is not the ugly, dark side of spiritual knowledge, witchcraft, divination, Ouija board, palm reading. Closing yourself to these illegitimate experiences through repentance is paramount. Open your heart to the indwelling presence of Jesus. Become familiar with His Person through the Word of God; yield to His leading, ask His Holy Spirit to lead and guide you into the Truth. For Truth is not a concept, precept, or way of thinking. Truth is a person. Jesus said in John 14:6, "I Am the Way, the Truth, and the Life…."

Come now! Read this book and allow the Lord to show you His glory, open up your spiritual sight—the eyes of your heart—and see.

> *Blessed [anticipating God's presence, spiritually mature] are the pure in heart [those with integrity, moral courage, and godly character], for they will see God.*
>
> Matthew 5:8 AMP

Definitions

Dark Place: An imprisoned or difficult situation needing light, hope, and input from Holy Spirit.

Debunk: Expose the falseness or hollowness of an idea, discredit, disprove.

Fourth Dimension: The realm of the spirit.

Imagination: From the word *image*. The place in us with ability to picture what isn't seen in the natural realm with the eyes of the heart.

Prophecy: Declaring the end from the beginning. Releasing God's perspective into the earth realm.

Prophetic Activation: Cause the prophetic gift of prophecy and/or seer to start functioning.

Prophetic Interpretation: The ability to perceive symbolic meaning from dreams and visions.

Prophetic Pictures: Scenes flashed on the lens of the heart that illustrate a present or future circumstance.

Seer: One who sees into the spirit realm and prophesies what is seen...In the Bible Gad, Iddo, and Asaph were seers. (From Paula A. Price, Ph.D. *The Prophet's Dictionary*.)

Seer: Possesses the ability to picture on the lens of the redeemed heart images from the fourth dimension, emphasis is on seeing rather than hearing.

Vision: A picture received on the lens of the eyes of the heart coming from the fourth dimension (spirit realm).

Foreword

DURING MY FORTY-PLUS YEARS OF MINISTRY, it has been a great blessing to know and work with numerous prophets. The prophetic anointing is invaluable. Proverbs 29:18 says that without "prophetic revelation" (a more accurate rendering of the word *chazown*, translated "vision" in the KJV) the people "perish." The Hebrew word translated *perish* also needs amplification; it carries a broad meaning. The word is *para* and can mean "naked or uncovered; unbridled or out of control; unprepared for opportunity; and more." The point of the verse is obvious: it is important to know what God is thinking and saying!

Whether it be running a business, ministering in the Church, raising children, praying, navigating relationships—it doesn't matter the area of life—the prophetic anointing helps bring success and life. I've never quite understood the theology saying God stopped communicating with His kids. His relational heart LONGS to communicate with us, as does any good parent. Whether through His word, the still small voice, prophecy, dreams or visions, God is a communicating God. Life is far more complicated and much less fulfilling when we do not hear from Him.

There are different types of prophets. In the same way that those called to teach and preach do so with different styles, through different personalities, and with a variety of giftings, the prophetic calling is also diverse. Some prophetic individuals are given more to dreams, others prophesy as the word bubbles up from their spirit, and still others see visions or pictures. Regina Shank is a mature "seer." As such, she is very qualified to teach on the subject.

Having worked with Regina for years, I've witnessed her keen ability to move in this gift. I've watched it in the apostolic center she leads, observed her functioning on prophetic presbyteries, and worked with her in larger groups on high-level prayer assignments. Her contributions are always significant and important. God frequently shows her pictures, impressions, insights, and direction which could not have been known without supernatural knowledge. Regina functions in this gift with maturity, not only "seeing" but skillfully interpreting and discerning appropriate action regarding what she sees. The result is always good fruit.

Those who've been around the prophetic for a while have, unfortunately, seen the weird and wild, which makes hearing from balanced and seasoned voices like Regina both refreshing and vitally important. She will not only help you mature in your "seeing" gift but in understanding what you see. She'll help you apply it accurately, and her gifting will awaken the gift in you—an often missed element in listening to those carrying certain anointings. I have absolutely no doubt that there are many to whom God has given prophetic gifts, including the "seer" gift, and yet they do not realize it.

You may be one of them. If so, I believe this book will awaken and activate the gift in you. Read it with expectation!

God is maturing the church. An increasing understanding of the prophetic gift is part of this process.

Foreword

As the growth occurs, we will represent Christ with more and more excellence, greater and greater productivity. Be a part of this!

Learn to listen. He IS speaking.

Dutch Sheets
Author and Speaker

1

The Spirit Realm

WE ARE BORN INTO a three-dimensional spatial world: height, depth, and width (plus time). Another dimension that was discovered and labeled by Einstein is the time dimension.

Yet another dimension exists where time and space have no influence. That dimension is the spirit realm. It is the realm where angels and demons affect our daily lives. Because that spiritual dimension is unseen by our natural eye, many do not acknowledge its existence. Others, without biblical input, open themselves up to the dark side of spiritual knowledge unaware of the repercussions of their actions. It is important to close any open doors of access to the dark side of the spirit realm through repentance prior to asking for activation of the gifts of the Spirit. Repentance is not only asking forgiveness for the act of initiating wrong input, but for accepting that input into our lives. In repenting, we make a total change of direction, a 180° turn towards God. If we do not shut those doors through repentance, that open door of demonic input can taint the gifts. This allows for a mixture rather than a pure flow from the Spirit of God. We are spirit beings, living in an earthly body, interacting with our world through our senses.

Dr. Paul Yonggi Cho, in his book *The Fourth Dimension*, gives definition to that realm of the spirit:

> The spirit is the fourth dimension. Every human being is a spiritual being as well as a physical being. They have the fourth dimension as well as the third dimension in their hearts... (pg. 39)
>
> Visions and dreams are the language of the fourth dimension, and the Holy Spirit communicates through them. (pg. 44)

The fourth dimension, the realm of the Spirit, is entered legitimately through Jesus Christ by the power of Holy Spirit. He is the door. When we look at Revelation 4:1, we see a pattern for entrance into the realm of the Spirit. "After this I looked, and there was a door open in heaven."

That door is Jesus. We cannot legally enter through any other means. If we do, the Bible says we are entering as thieves and robbers.

Jesus speaks of himself and mentions thieves and robbers in John 10: 1, 7-9:

> *"I tell you the truth, the man who does not enter the sheep pen by the gate, but climbs in by some other way, is a thief and a robber..."*

Therefore Jesus said again, "I tell you the truth, I am the gate (door) for the sheep. All who ever came before me were thieves and robbers, but the sheep did not listen to them. I am the gate (door); whoever enters through me will be saved. He will come in and go out and find pasture."

The curtain between the outer court and the Holy of Holies was torn in two when Jesus, through His sacrifice, restored access to a personal relationship with God.

In I Samuel 28, we have the historical account of King Saul consulting a witch for input into his life and position. Contacting the dead is forbidden in scripture. The Egyptian magicians in Moses' day could perform signs, but their source was illegitimate. Seeking fallen angels for spiritual information will cause the lens of the eyes of our heart to become clouded at the very least.

Some time ago, I had a dream in which an acquaintance who had passed away, appeared to me. Yet all was not right. This person in my dream had a resemblance to the one who had passed on but did not speak as they did, nor did they give me counsel that lined up with the word of God.

I rejected that dream, realizing it was not the Lord who had allowed it. It was a demonic force projecting itself through a dream, trying to gain entrance into my life.

Discerning the source of spiritual information is key to walking in the purity of God's spiritual input. Another key is knowing the voice and Word of God.

If you have been in banking, you know the proper way to discern counterfeit bills is to know and become acquainted with the genuine. Knowing the Lord and His voice, knowing the Word of God, knowing Holy Spirit will keep us on track with the genuine voice of God. The only door into the Spirit realm that is legitimate is Jesus by the power of Holy Spirit.

Back to Revelation 4:

And the voice I had first heard speaking to me like a trumpet, said…

We listen to His voice, inviting us into fellowship with Him for encouragement, direction, edification, impartation and just plain fellowship. We have the opportunity to respond to that voice. We can have several responses:

- We can choose to come through the door and hear what the Lord has to say to me.
- We can question the source of that voice, and so not respond.
- We can choose not to respond at all because I am unsure how to do so.

When we hear His voice, it requires a response.

Revelation 4:

"Come up here, and I will show you what must take place after this."

When the Lord invites us into a realm we have not entered before, we are being offered legitimate entrance through Jesus. When His voice gives us an invitation, a response is necessary. We can choose to accept His invitation or remain in our present state of intimacy with Him.

> *After this I looked, and there before me was a door standing open in heaven. And the voice I had first heard speaking to me like a trumpet said, "Come up here, and I will show you what must take place after this."*
>
> Revelation 4:1

That throne is described in several places in the Word of God, but we will look at Isaiah 6:1-8:

> *In the year that King Uzziah died, I saw the Lord, high and exalted, seated on a throne; and the train of his robe filled the temple. Above him were seraphim, each with six wings: With two wings they covered their faces, with two they covered their feet, and with two they were flying. And they were calling to one another: "Holy, holy, holy is the Lord Almighty; the whole earth is full of his glory. At the sound of their voices the doorposts and thresholds shook, and the temple was filled with smoke "Woe to me!" I cried. "I am ruined! For I am a man of unclean lips, and I live among a people of unclean lips, and my eyes have seen the King, the Lord Almighty." Then one of the seraphim flew to me with a live coal in his hand, which he had taken with tongs from the altar. With it he touched my mouth and said, "See, this has touched your lips; your guilt is taken away and your sin atoned for." Then I heard the voice of the Lord saying, "Whom shall I send? And who will go for us? "And I said, "Here am I. Send me!"*

I realize this is Isaiah's commissioning as a prophet. It is also an experience that changed his life and thrust him into a realm of the spirit the dimension(s) that affects the four dimensions we experience in the natural realm. Activating the Seer Realm opens up experiences, sights, sounds, and earthly impact from that realm by the power of encounters and revelation from Holy Spirit. Notice that Isaiah encounters the throne with someone sitting on it. I personally believe that throne is in our hearts. We are carriers of the Lord's presence. If we have not allowed the Lord to occupy His own throne, we have negated our ability to go deeper into the spiritual realm.

> *Deep calls to deep in the roar of your waterfalls; all your waves and breakers have swept over me.*
>
> Psalms 42:7

We are the mobile temple of Holy Spirit.

> *Do you not know that your bodies are temples of the Holy Spirit, who is in you, whom you have received from God? You are not your own; you were bought at a price. Therefore, honor God with your bodies.*
>
> I Corinthians 6:19-20

These are not merely historical stories in the Word of God, but they are experiences we too can enter into. To do so, we must overcome our preconceived ideas about their reality, our doctrinal input that negates such experience, and our own reluctance and/or fear to allow our spirit man to encounter the Spirit of God in such a manner. So, let's proceed further into the seer realm and learn how to access its riches.

GRANDMA'S GARDEN

I remember springtime at the family farm in Missouri. When the ground warmed up, it was time to prepare the soil for planting. My grandmother was the matriarch of the family. (My grandfather passed away at the age of 52.) She knew how to do nearly everything. I was the second oldest grandchild and stayed with Grandma at least two weeks each spring and summer. Our southwest Missouri farm had been in the family for at least 100 years.

After the original house burnt to the ground, a new house was needed. The basement of the present home had been dug out by a team of horses. The smokehouse was an essential structure in those days and housed the meat from the cattle and pigs. But the dark, rich soil of the farm impressed me most with its ability to bring forth amazing harvests. That garden plot produced an abundant crop of vegetables year after year. It had become an annual task to remove the rocks, pull the weeds, plow the rows, and plant the seeds that would sprout, grow, and bring forth what was anticipated.

It was my job to find the rocks and throw them over the fence. I loved helping my grandmother, but pulling weeds, throwing rocks over the fence, plowing, and planting didn't appear to be a fun afternoon to me. I was grumbling about my job, when Grandma started describing what was to come.

A side note—my name is Regina, but Grandma called me, "Susie." I never knew why she had that pet name for me, but she liked it, and I grew to like it. Not another person in my life called me Susie, but grandma. Excuse the digression, now onto the story.

The Seer Gift

As I looked at the patch of garden, all I could see was Missouri dirt filled with weeds and rocks, and an abundance of work in the hot sun. But Grandma saw something else. She saw green beans, corn, watermelon, onions, lettuce, potatoes, and cucumbers. The eyes of her heart were seeing the unseen future of a patch of dirt and rocks in a fertile valley next to the branch (a pure, clean tiny stream). She pictured what was coming. She saw the end from the beginning. She described what was to come, using her imagination to help me picture what wasn't there. She saw it; I didn't. She sketched it out for me.

Over here, pointing to the left corner of the garden, we will have watermelon. I know you like that. I've seen you eat it. And over here, we will have corn. I know you like corn-on-the-cob with lots of butter and salt. Can't you see what we are doing?

I reluctantly said, "yes." Then turned my eyes to the rocks, dirt, and weeds that were blocking my view. My heart wasn't fully engaged with Grandma's picture. I couldn't "see" her corn and watermelon. To me, they weren't there yet. But I could picture myself playing in the cool, clear water of the branch that flowed through the valley. It was hot in this Missouri sunshine.

Grandma pictured her yet-to-be garden. I pictured my potential future playing in the stream. Both of us pictured what we hoped was our future. We saw, not with our natural eyes, but with the eyes of our heart, what we dreamed about.

Most of us think a dream is some kind of video playing in our minds as we sleep. But don't forget daydreams! I was notorious for fading out of my surroundings and being somewhere else in my thoughts. I could picture myself on the playground while sitting in my desk in 3rd grade. I could picture myself exploring abandoned houses, climbing a mountain, riding my bike, all the while sitting in my desk at school or on a pew at church.

This is where the seer gift comes from. It is not an apparition or an out-of-the-body experience, although I know those are possible. It is simply seeing with the eyes of our redeemed imagination what the Lord is revealing. If you can picture something, you have just accessed the "eyes of your heart." The seer gift starts with the ability to picture what isn't there in the natural realm but seen with vision by the spirit. The key to sorting through these pictures is discerning the source of them.

Both Grandma and I could see what our hearts desired. She desired produce from her garden; I desired to play in the creek. Dreams placed within us give birth to vision for our future. Dreams placed within us by the Spirit of God give birth to insight, hope, and encouragement for others and open up our ability to see what God is revealing. By the way, Grandma got her garden, and I got my dream of playing the creek.

2

Dreams and Visions

Seer Experience

> *But blessed are your eyes because they see, and your ears because they hear. For I tell you the truth, many prophets and righteous men longed to see what you see, but did not see it, and to hear what you hear but did not hear it.*
>
> Matthew 13:16-17 NET

SHE CAME TO MY CLASS HUNGERING FOR FREEDOM. I could see it in her demeanor; she was fearful yet hopeful for an encounter with the God who loved her. Suddenly, her life unfolded before me in a vision. I "saw" her life as a squeezebox, an instrument that collapses, but when pulled apart makes a sound that, when played properly, is beautiful. I began to prophesy the squeezebox vision into her life.

"Your life has been very difficult. You have all but collapsed from the overwhelming circumstances in your life. The pressure has been too much, but the Lord loves you and is bringing you into restoration."

She began to cry. Her emotions poured out as the picture I described spoke to her.

I continued.

"There is a sound that the Lord wants to release out of you, a sound of restoration, a sound of hope, a sound of healing."

Another picture flashed in my mind. I saw (or pictured) a younger woman. The Lord had His hand on her head, turning her completely around.

I asked the woman in front of me, 'Do you have a daughter?'

'Yes,' she said quietly through her tears."

I continued to prophesy.

"The Lord is going to turn her life around. She is going to turn from her present lifestyle, rejecting it for a relationship with Jesus. Keep praying. Your prayers are making a difference. Your daughter will come to the end of herself and find Jesus waiting to embrace her."

This mother continued to cry over the joy received from the words spoken to her. She had been praying for her daughter for quite some time. Our team prayed for both of them, speaking in agreement with what was seen in the visions, decreeing the future of God's purpose.

The Lord provided these visions to give this woman hope for change, hope that her life would not always be the same, hope and faith that her prayers were reaching heaven and an answer was on the way. The seer gift coupled with the prophetic gift brought forth light in a dark situation. What was seen in the spirit realm was released prophetically to give her light (revelation) in a dark place.

> *So we have the prophetic word made sure, to which you do well to pay attention as to a lamp shining in a dark place, until the day dawns and the morning star arises in your hearts. But know this first of all, that no prophecy of Scripture is a matter of one's own interpretation, for no prophecy was ever made by an act of human will, but men moved by the Holy Spirit spoke from God.*
>
> 2 Peter 1:19 -21 NASB

Imagine yourself sitting in a dark room, feeling hemmed in by overwhelming circumstances. Hopelessness has captured you, and despair is sitting next to you. Suddenly, a word of prophecy from the Spirit of God breaks into your darkness bringing light into your situation. The dark room is no longer dark. The seer gift has turned on a lamp, showing the end from the beginning. That lamp, prophetic vision, gave hope that your situation will change.

The Lord loves His creation and does not want us to sit in a dark situation, void of hope for the future, but desires to bring light into that darkness. Darkness can block the road ahead and cause paralysis in a situation that looks and/or feels permanent. The scripture in 2 Peter describes the prophetic word as a lamp shining in a dark place.

I remember helping an older relative see. Her vision in the natural was impaired during an accident she experienced as a little girl. Due to the injury, she wore thick glasses and this became a major reason she never learned to drive. At times, I became her eyes. She trusted me to get her where she needed to go. The prophetic word is like that. It can lead us out of a place of impaired spiritual vision. The seer gift is not for the seer; it is for those who cannot see their way forward in a dark situation. Without the light of the prophetic word, the loss of vision for the future traps us in a hopeless situation.

The seer gift has the ability to see and reveal the end from the beginning.

> *Declaring the end and the result from the beginning, and from ancient times the things which have not yet been done, Saying, 'My purpose will be established, and I will do all that please Me and fulfills My purpose.'*
>
> Isaiah 46:10 AMP

The seer gift, by the power of Holy Spirit, sees a vision of victory and plants hope for breakthrough. The word spoken from the seer realm becomes a light that dispels darkness and gives hope and provides forward movement toward recovery. The prophetic vision, declared in prophecy, turns on a lamp, enough light to illumine darkness and hopefully sustain the receiver on the journey to restoration.

The rest of the verse in 2 Peter 1:19-21 says:

> *Until the day dawns and the morning star arises in your hearts.*

When day dawns, night is over. Here is an example that illustrates this principle.

A very prophetic friend of mine, Clay Nash, envisioned me wearing a coat that was too large for me. He prophesied to me. He even said it was my Father's coat that I had not grown into yet. He declared that I would continue to grow into the anointing or mantle that the Lord had given me. I knew he was referring to my Father God who had mantled me for His calling on my life. What Clay did not know is that when my father died, I got his coat. Soon after that I led a prayer team to China and chose to wear my dad's large coat as a representation of wearing the mantle of Father God. The coat was indeed too large for me, but I wore it anyway. The seer gift operating in my friend who knew nothing of the coat, encouraged me to pursue from Father God the ability to grow into the mantle I had been given. It was illustrated in the natural by the coat of my father, yet represented the mantle of my Father God. I have grown since that time, and the coat/mantle in the Spirit fits better than my dad's coat.

The day dawning in 2 Peter 1:21 represents the fulfillment of the prophetic word, the seer vision, the purpose of God in our lives.

DREAMS

The seer gift includes both visions (pictures that flash on the screen of the eyes of your heart while you are awake), and dreams (night visions that occur during sleep.)

Years ago, a very prophetic friend of mine passed away. He was gifted with the ability to spiritually see the end from the beginning and prophesy into situations affecting people and ministries. After he had left this earth, in a night vision (a dream), he sat next to me at a food bar in a restaurant. He asked me if I would receive his prophetic mantle. He was disappointed that he didn't get to finish his purpose on the earth and wanted to pass it on to me. In this dream, I responded that I would be honored to receive and carry that gift along with what the Lord had already given me to steward. In this night vision, I was given a new mantle.

The online dictionary defines mantle as: "an important role or responsibility that passes from one person to another." I agree with that definition, but biblically, it includes not only the responsibility but the empowerment to carry it out.

I looked at the Word of God to confirm the viability of this encounter. The account of Elijah and Elisha gave credence to my dream. The NIV calls the mantle a cloak.

> *Elisha then picked up Elijah's cloak that had fallen from him and went back and stood on the bank of the Jordan. He took the cloak that had fallen from Elijah and struck the water with it. "Where now is the Lord, the God of Elijah?" he asked. When he struck the water, it divided to the right and to the left, and he crossed over.*
>
> *The company of the prophets from Jericho, who were watching, said, "The spirit of Elijah is resting on Elisha." And they went to meet him and bowed to the ground before him.*
>
> 2 Kings 2:13-15

Night visions are one aspect of the seer gift. Many people dismiss these dreams with a blanket statement (sic) such as, "everybody dreams." But dreams must be stewarded, processed, written down, and prayed over. Sharing those dreams with other gifted individuals for their interpretation can bring insight that the Lord is imparting through them. I point seekers to the book of Daniel.

I love the following scripture.

> *In the first year of Belshazzar king of Babylon, Daniel had a dream, and visions passed through his mind as he was lying in bed. He wrote down the substance of his dream.*
>
> Daniel 7:1

I believe Daniel understood the source of his dreams was the Spirit of God, and he also knew they were important enough to write down and process. Being a good steward over your dreams will open the door for more input from the Spirit of God. When we express faith in little, the Lord will trust us with more.

One night I had a dream. In the dream, a woman had strewn straight pins all over the floor of a bedroom. There was a baby lying on the floor on top of these pins. I could see the baby bed in the room. But the baby was not safe lying on the floor with sharp objects all around him. I knew in my spirit that it was a warning dream for a baby. I didn't know who the baby was but prayed for the child in my dream.

Later that day, my son called me and said they had called 911 because his son, my grandson, had choked on the formula in his bottle and was not breathing. I knew instantly that the dream I had the night before was about this incident. After my son called, I prayed for our baby with two other people. We decreed over him that he would live and not die, that he would come back into his body and live out the destiny the Lord had designed for him. After about 15-20 minutes, my son called back and said, "Mom, he came back. The emergency personnel were able to clear his windpipe and he is breathing. We thought he was gone, but he came back, and his breathing is restored."

The exact prayer we had prayed for my grandson came out of my son's mouth. He had not heard us pray, but the Lord certainly did.

"He came back."

The warning dream I had the night before and the prayer we prayed for the baby in my dream was playing out before our eyes. I believe that warning dream saved my grandson. I pay attention to my dreams.

ACTIVATION

Lord,

Help me to be a faithful steward over my dreams, discerning their source, and processing what the Spirit is depositing within me. I repent for not taking my dreams seriously. I have been guilty of apathy towards these night visions. All the while, you could be releasing answers to my prayers, keys to open new doors or shut off access to the enemy. I ask you to restore what I have ignored. I chose to pay attention to your input while I am sleeping.

I want to be like Daniel who wrote down and pondered his dreams, receiving insight previously unknown.

    Amen.

3

🗝 Purity of Heart

SEVERAL YEARS AGO, WE SANG A SONG in our worship services that voiced the cry for a clean heart. "Refiner's Fire" by Brian Doerksen. The lyrics are a prayer, a cry for purity of heart.

> *Purify my heart*
> *Let me be as gold and precious silver*
> *Purify my heart*
> *Let me be as gold, pure gold, Lord*
> *Let me be as gold, pure gold*
> *Refiner's fire*
> *My heart's one desire*
> *Is to be holy*
> *Set apart for You, Lord*
> *I choose to be holy*
> *Set apart for You, my Master*
> *Ready to do Your will*
> *Purify my heart*

Cleanse me from within
And make me holy
Purify my heart
Cleanse me from my sin
Deep within
Refiner's fire
My heart's one desire
Is to be holy
Set apart for You, Lord
I choose to be holy
Set apart for You, my Master
Ready to do Your will

"Refiner's Fire" is a cry of the heart to be purified. The Lord alone is able to discern the condition of our hearts.

According to Jeremiah 17:9-10 NASB:

> *The heart is more deceitful than all else and is desperately sick; Who can understand it? I, the Lord, search the heart, I test the mind, even to give to each man according to his ways, according to the results of his deeds.*

And in Matthew 5:8:

> *Blessed are the pure in heart, for they shall see God.*

A few years ago, we were driving home from Kansas City in a snowstorm. Our car windshield was covered with snow, and ice began to form more quickly than the defrost system could handle. The combination of sleet, ice, and snow made it impossible to see the road in front of us. We had to pull over on the side of the road and use our scraper to scrape the ice from the windshield. The rear window was covered as well, so by the time we had removed the ice from both windows, it was beginning to form again. Needless to say, we had a difficult time getting home. The ability to see the road was crucial. Without a clean windshield, our vision was hindered to the degree that we were stuck by the side of the road.

The same is true with spiritual vision. The eyes of the heart are affected by what we allow ourselves to gaze upon. Psalm 101:3 (NASB) says: "I will set no worthless thing before my eyes…" When we look at things such as pornography, movies that put vile scenes on the inner screen of our heart, we are in essence covering our spiritual eyes with a film that must be removed through repentance. Repentance cleanses the eyes of the heart and allows the screen to be clear and clean again. Repentance is the Windex on the window of the soul. Repentance is not just, "I'm sorry." It is a change of mind and heart.

Perhaps we have never warmed up to the possibility of "seeing in the Spirit." It has been said that we see things as we are, not as they are. Also, unforgiveness, anger, resentment, offense, religious judgments, rebellion can coat our hearts with a sheet of ice that must be removed in order to clear our spiritual vision. From Matthew 5:8,

We know that the pure of heart see God. I believe it means we can see his perspective; we can see His heart for us and for others.

Sin can be like ice on the windshield of the heart or a dirty film on the glass, blocking the potential for spiritual vision. The spiritual eyes become blocked or dim at best.

Recently we were driving home from a visit with our children when we noticed our windshield was getting very dirty. We turned on the windshield wipers and the washer fluid to clean the front glass. It had been raining and the dirt on the glass mixed with the gentle rain had proceeded to block our vision. We found that the passenger side of the glass was clean and clear because the washer fluid was working and sprayed its liquid while the wipers did the rest. The driver's side however was still dirty because there was a clog in the fluid dispenser. It was not easy to see the road ahead with rain coming down and a film blocking my vision. I was the driver and realized we had to clear the dirt that was blocking our vision, in order to proceed on our journey. What should be working was not working because of the clog in the dispenser. It left me with no alternative but to take desperate measures. We had to exit the vehicle, get soaking wet from the rain, find a cloth to wipe the dirt from the window, and then return to the vehicle.

Just like the windshield, our hearts can become clogged with trauma, unforgiveness, wrong perceptions, or a bad experience with church life. Sometimes ministry is required to remove layers of false perceptions, traumas, and the result of sinful actions. A pure heart is key to seeing clearly. How do we get the windshield of our hearts clean? It starts with an appeal to the Lord.

King David certainly had his share of opportunities to see life through a dirty lens. After all, the King Saul threw a spear at him and sought to kill him. David had to run for his life. The Amalekites robbed him of all his possessions including his family. His brothers were jealous of him, mocked him and did not recognize his destiny. But David was a man after God's heart. He knew that his own heart had to remain clean in order to receive, with clarity, the direction of the Lord. I love King David's prayer in Psalm 51:10-17 NASB:

> *Create in me a pure heart, O God, and renew a steadfast spirit within me. Do not cast me from your presence or take your Holy Spirit from me. Restore to me the joy of your salvation and grant me a willing spirit, to sustain me. Then I will teach transgressors your ways, so that sinners will turn back to you. Deliver me from the guilt of bloodshed, O God, you who are God my Savior, and my tongue will sing of your righteousness. Open my lips, Lord and my mouth will declare your praise. You do not delight in sacrifice, or I would bring it; you do not take pleasure in burnt offerings. My sacrifice, O God, is a broken spirit; a broken and contrite heart you, God, will not despise.*

ACTIVATION

We can pray the prayer of King David printed above. If this one does not speak to you, here is an additional prayer to cleanse the heart.

Lord,

Purify our hearts from the road dust of past journeys. Keep us from seeing things through the lens of trauma, hurt, painful relationships, or unholy things we have allowed our eyes to see. Purify the eyes of my heart and the lens of my soul. I want to see you and all that you want

The Seer Gift

to project through me for the benefit of others. I give you permission to use your windshield cleanser on me. I want to see clearly the road ahead and be able to help others in their journey as well.

Amen.

4

Perspective

IT HAS BEEN SAID, "SEEING IS BELIEVING!" But I have found that statement to be less than true, especially when referring to the gift of seeing in the spirit. Many people who have not perceived their spiritual sense of sight have ignored or dismissed momentary glimpses into that realm. We tend to label people who have the gift of spiritual sight, seers, or in some circles, schizophrenic. Which one is it? Are these people mentally unstable or could they be spiritually gifted to see what the natural eye is incapable of? Or could it be that we all have the ability to see spiritually, but it has not been activated, understood, or received as possible? It depends on your perspective, which generally has been formed by your way of thinking. The Bible tells us that we are transformed by the renewing of our minds. See Romans 12:1-2.

We actually have a team of seers in our ministry. This team is able to see pictures, scenes, Court of Heaven activity, visions of historic episodes in people's lives, angels, demons, future events, and when released, visions of heaven, the cloud of witnesses, and more. Angelic visitations are not outside their experience.

Why would anyone want a gift so controversial? It can be misused, flaunted, resisted, misjudged, coveted, mocked, or valued. Yet, even though controversial, our team of seers is called by people from all over the world! Why are they seeking the manifestation of a gift so misunderstood or ignored by much of Christendom? The answer is: they are seeking answers to life's problems. Perhaps they tried other sources and in desperation turned to Jesus, looking for answers not found by natural means. The Lord is faithful and true. He wants to give breakthrough. Our leader, Jesus by the power of Holy Spirit, can bring that breakthrough.

> *Your leader will break out and lead you out of exile, out through the gates of the enemy cities, back to your own land. Your king will lead you; the Lord himself will guide you.*
>
> Micah 2:13 NLT

We cannot reduce the Word of God to mental understanding or logic and reason. The Word of God was given to reach the heart of man. The Holy Spirit was given to do the same. When Adam and Eve partook of the forbidden fruit in Genesis, the tree of the knowledge of good and evil entered into their DNA and man became intellectually led, limited to his own understanding and perceptions, cut off from the input of spiritual understanding and wisdom. Separated from God, and in their fallen state, they were cut off from the tree of life

Perspective

which would have allowed them to live forever in that condition. We can look at that event and see it as a terrible thing, and it was, but worse yet would have been mankind relegated to live forever cut off from the Spirit of God. God in His mercy cut off man's access to the tree of life. I agree with God; we would not want to live forever in a fallen state.

From the foundation of the world, the Lord had a plan to bring man back to His Presence and wisdom. That plan was Jesus. Jesus came in the midst of time to bring us back to God, restoring access to the Tree of Life and the wisdom received from it. We have a choice to make. We can choose to continue eating of the tree of the knowledge of good and evil, making decisions from an intellectual perspective, cut off from the Tree of Life, or we can live by religious concepts, doing our best to be and do good things so we can earn the reward of eternal life. Either of these decisions cuts us off from the revealed insight of heaven. Jesus said in John 14:6, "I am the way, the Truth, and the Life." The tree of life is the only choice that connects us back to God. That tree of life is Jesus.

Jesus said in John 17:3 NASB, "This is eternal life, that they may know You, the only true God, and Jesus Christ whom You have sent."

Eternal life is knowing God and Jesus Christ. It is not earned by our behavior. That concept comes from the tree of knowledge of good and evil. Life is a gift of God. It is not earned. If you have not received that gift of righteousness and eternal life, you can ask for it from the Father, through the sacrifice of His Son on the cross. He bought you back from your fallen state, redeemed you from being relegated to your own devices. You can now have access to all of God's wisdom, insight, and direction through relationship with Jesus and the Holy Spirit who purposes to give insight and direction for your life and reveal Jesus to and through you.

A.W. Tozer in his book, *Mystery of the Holy Spirit* writes: "the realm of the Spirit is closed to the intellect. It is not difficult to understand why. You see the spirit is the organ by which we apprehend divine things, and the human spirit is dead because of sin. Therefore, the human intellect is not the organ by which we apprehend divine things."

The life of God can flow through your being, opening the eyes of the heart. Those spiritual eyes are not opened until Jesus takes up residence as Lord and Savior. Jesus can then sit on the throne of the heart, leading by His Spirit and redeeming our lives from having to live by our limited faulty knowledge.

I remember living my life trying to earn God's approval. I HAD to go to church every Sunday. I HAD to be a "good" person. My thoughts were, "Only good people go to heaven, so I will try to be good: wear the right clothes, listen to the right music, run with the right friends, please the people around me." It was too difficult to achieve. Being good is not possible.

Jesus said, "Why do you call me good?" Jesus answered. "No one is good—except God alone." Mark 10:18

So many times, I have heard people say, "They are good people."

<u>*Perspective*</u>

Good people don't go to heaven. Neither Heaven nor a relationship with God is earned by our goodness. I remember someone saying to me, we have to be good. I asked the question, "When do you know that you are good enough?"

Their answer was, "Not until you die and stand before God."

I looked at that person and said, "I can't follow you or your perception of salvation. You are lost."

As a young believer, working through this dilemma of grace versus works was difficult for me. So many people around me were telling me how good I had to be. Remember the phrase from the Christmas song, Santa Claus is coming to town: "You better watch out. You better not cry. You better not pout…He's making a list, He's checking it twice, Gonna find out who's naughty or nice…So be good for goodness' sake."

At that time, I was also going to a church that preached good behavior and salvation through the blood of Jesus. It was a message that emphasized "…Work out your salvation with fear and trembling." Philippians 2:12

> *For by grace you have been saved through faith. And this is not your own doing; it is the gift of God, not a result of works, so that no one may boast. For we are his workmanship, created in Christ Jesus for good works, which God prepared beforehand, that we should walk in them.*
>
> Ephesians 2:8-10 ESV

I was attending college in that season of my life. I remember praying as I was driving, asking the Lord to show me in a big way which one of those diametrically opposing views was correct.

"Is it works or grace? I'm tired of trying so hard to please you. I can't do this anymore! Who is right?"

As soon as I got this prayer out of my mouth, I saw a large semi-tractor truck coming down the road toward me. On the side of the large trailer were the words, "GRACE."

I knew the Lord was answering my desperate prayer. I began to weep, finding a deep release from the works mentality that had held me in bondage for so long. I received His grace on another level and asked Him to lead and guide me in my life. After this, I continued to "run into" scriptures that released me from my performance Christianity and my works mentality. I found out I did not have to earn His gifts, nor His approval. I was approved because I received the grace of His sacrifice for me. This opened up a new trust in me to allow Him to bring forth the fruits of the Spirit in my life; that became a foundation for the release of the gifts as well. He opened up the eyes of my heart to "see" Him not as a demanding Savior, but as a loving Father. May the Lord give you a "spirit of wisdom and revelation in the knowledge of Him."

> *For this reason I too, having heard of the faith in the Lord Jesus which exists among you and your love for all the saints, do not cease giving thanks for you, while making mention of you in my prayers; that the God of our Lord Jesus Christ, the Father of glory, may give to you a spirit of wisdom and of revelation in the knowledge of Him. I pray that the eyes of your heart may be*

enlightened, so that you will know what is the hope of His calling, what are the riches of the glory of His inheritance in the saints, and what is the surpassing greatness of His power toward us who believe.

Ephesians 1:15-19 NASB

ACTIVATION

Lord,

I ask you to restore my Spiritual sight, to open my eyes to see the glorious inheritance I have in you. I know from scripture that when I receive you, I am eating of the Tree of Life. I no longer have to exclusively depend on my own thoughts or my own good ideas. Thank you for restoring access to your wisdom, guidance, and direction in my life. Forgive me for telling you my good ideas and asking you to bless them. Forgive me for trying to perform to please you. You paid the price for my sin and brought me back into relationship with you through the blood of your Son. Through you I have access to the tree of life who is Jesus. Open my spiritual eyes to see what I could not see previously. I agree with your word in Ephesians that you will open the eyes of my heart. Once I was blind, now I want to see.

Amen.

5

⚷ Misconceptions Debunked

LET'S DEBUNK A FEW MISCONCEPTIONS about the seer gift. (**Debunk:** expose the falseness or hollowness of an idea.)

Well-meaning people have rejected the ability to see with the eyes of the heart thinking It is a mystic trance or entrance into La La land. It is neither, nor is it a result of being overpowered to the degree that we lose control of our normal senses. Don't get me wrong, I'm sure those things can happen whether sourced by the power of Holy Spirit or through previous dabbling into witchcraft and/or demonic doors opened through disobedience to God's Word. The dark side of spiritual knowledge must be cleansed through repentance and deliverance. Because that is not the focus of this book, I encourage you to purchase and read my book called, Deliverance to

Freedom available on my website: www.reginashank.com, and pray through the last chapter that contains the Freedom Map. These prayers of repentance cleanse the lens of the soul, much like cleaning the windshield of the ice-covered car. This makes it possible to see the road ahead and allow Holy Spirit opportunity to project clear and genuine pictures on the eyes of our hearts.

Jesus warned of the enemy's tactics and decreed that there was no place in Him for the enemy to access. Access points, possible because of doors of demonic ingress unrepented of, allow mixed images to enter into our imagery.

> *I will not talk with you much more, for the prince (evil genius, ruler) of the world is coming. And he has no claim on Me. [He has nothing in common with Me; there is nothing in Me that belongs to him, and he has no power over Me.*
>
> John 14:30 AMPC

When I was a teenager, I would occasionally go to a small indoor movie theatre operating in our city. A blind man, who was familiar to me because of his cane, brown overcoat and frequent afternoon walks around the town square, would visit the theatre as well. I was amazed at his ability to navigate his surroundings. His cane stretched out in front of him, searching for obstacles that might be in his path. He wore sunglasses to cover his eyes, not because of glare, but to shield the observer from the blank stare in his unseeing eyes. He navigated his surroundings with such ease that those of us depending on our eyes rather than our other senses marveled at his expertise. Even more surprising was a blind man who chose to "watch" a movie! He would get his ticket (I don't think they charged him for it because of his handicap), enter the theatre, find his seat on the back row, to see and listen to the movie. I would see him back there, curious as to how a movie entertained a man with no ability to see in the natural. Did he just listen without picturing the scenes on the screen? Did he see with the eyes of his heart the unfolding drama floating in giant panorama scenes in front of me? Perhaps he used his seer gift, the eyes of his heart, to picture what was on the screen. He may have used this ability for all of his daily activities. This man navigated his life by his inward ability to picture what was there, but not seen.

"How do you see in the Spirit realm?" It's easier than you think.

Even as natural blindness is real, spiritual blindness is also real. If I were blind in the natural realm, I would not see what is right in front of me. My inability to see would not negate the fact that there are objects, people, landscapes, cities, etc. to be seen. They are there, but my capacity for sight, plants doubt in their existence. It is the same with spiritual sight. If the eyes of my heart have not been enlightened, the darkened state gives excuse to deny the existence of the spiritual realm. It is like a blind man groping in the darkness for something solid to confirm a reality that evades his visual perception. Our minds tell us, if it cannot be seen, heard, or felt, then it doesn't exist. Much of Christendom lives in this dilemma, claiming the impossibility of spiritual experience, because it has not been experienced personally.

That phrase "eyes of the heart" is not symbolic or poetic, but an actual gift activated in the spiritual realm to see the unseen. In its purest form, it is designed to show you who you really are as a Spirit being, living in an earthly body, perceiving the natural realm through your mind and emotions, but also activating your spiritual eyes to see what the Lord is capable of revealing. The Lord wants to reveal Himself to and through you. If you do not believe He can or will do this, the seeking is over. You are relegated to a Christian life without the experience of a personal God, who not only talks to His children and reveals Himself to them, but also speaks through visions and dreams. We don't have too much trouble believing in dreams. We all have them. Many of us have visions as well, but we do not recognize them as such. Accessing the spirit realm by the power of Holy Spirit is a gift given to all who have received Holy Spirit. Many have denied the moving of the Spirit, possibly because it is not understood or received by the intellect. If we do not believe something is possible, we do not pursue it. False concepts, belief systems that have been sown into us by well-meaning but uninformed people, have to be overcome in order to access what we previously thought impossible.

    I personally love Bible study. The Word is so precious to me, but it is not meant to be one dimensional: designed to be read and gleaned only by the intellect of man. Holy Spirit wrote the scripture Himself through inspired men. You can read the Word like you read a textbook, gaining knowledge, reading stories, memorizing names, dates, entire chapters of the Bible. I have done that. That is what I was "trained" to do. I could tell you the names of the two wives of Elkanah, quote the entire first chapter of James, name the books of the Bible in order, divide them into categories of major prophets, minor prophets etc. In other words, I knew the Bible, but I did not know the Bible was alive, even though Hebrews 4:12 said so.

For the word of God is living and powerful, and sharper than any two-edged sword, piercing even to the division of soul and spirit, and of joints and marrow, and is a discerner of the thoughts and intents of the heart.

Hebrews 4:12 NKJV

If the Word is alive—and it is—it can speak to us personally. If God is alive—and He is—why would He quit speaking to His people? There are those who believe the Bible is a history book of God's dealings with His people. It's as if they say, "That's all there is folks. One of these days Jesus will come again, and you better be ready, but if you don't toe the line, go to church every Sunday, or at least on Easter—the day we worship the goddess Ishtar and roll her eggs around to entertain the children—then you are going to go to hell."

(Oops! I think I might have caused a rumble preceding an earthquake in the area of theology. Personally, I have trouble naming Resurrection Day—the day Jesus rose from the grave, conquering death, hell and grave—after a foreign goddess.)

OK, here's a less-controversial version:

"Yes, I know Jesus died on the cross for you, but you better be a good person. If you sin right before you die, and you haven't repented of it, that sin will send you to hell."

Where do we get this stuff???

Some are still in kindergarten (perhaps all of us), when it comes to knowing God and making Him known. It's not about performance or knowledge; It's about relationship with a Father who loved His creation so much that He sent His only Son to die on our behalf. Jesus restored the personal relationship with the Father. He restored the voice of God in our lives. Without His voice, we are limited to our own intellect, separated from the wisdom of the Tree of Life. Because of what Jesus did, paying the redemption for our sin, we no longer have to send Moses up to hear God for us. God can and does speak to His children. In Genesis 3:8, Adam and Eve heard the Lord in the garden of Eden. They had just sinned and hid themselves from the Lord because of their disobedience.

> *And they heard the sound of the Lord God walking in the garden in the cool of the day, and Adam and his wife hid themselves from the presence of the Lord God among the trees of the garden.*
>
> Genesis 3:8 NKJV

When you research the word *heard* in the *Strong's Concordance*, you find this definition: "a primitive root; to hear intelligently (often with implication of {attention} {obedience}, etc.; causatively to {tell| etc.) ..."

As I meditate on the word *heard* in Genesis 3:8, I realize that when we hear the sound of God, it requires a response of obedience or a withdrawal from His Presence. We are drawn to His Word or we hide ourselves from Him. Have we hidden ourselves from His Presence because of disobedience to His voice? In our churches and gatherings that carry His Name, have we gone through the motions of worship, preaching, prayer, with no regard for His Presence. Do we know "how" to do church, so we don't need Him?

I was perusing through an old hymnal that I found in my collection of piano music. I was surprised to see an order of worship that had been approved by the leaders of that denomination. It was all laid out for them. There was no need to engage the heart. There was no need to hear from the Lord. It was if to say: "Here is the ritual. Do it and God will be pleased this week."

I thought of the scripture.

This people honors me with their lips, but their heart is far away from me.

Matthew 15:8 NASB

The Lord wants relationship, not ritualistic recitations. I believe God wants His church back. We demonstrate that we don't need Him by our ability to have services that He is not a part of. We cut ourselves off from His Presence as Adam and Eve did. Could the blind be leading the blind, and we are all falling into the ditch of lack of personal and corporate spiritual input?

SEER EXPERIENCE

Several years ago, I was sitting in a church service about half-way back from the front of the building. I was facing the front, when I turned around to look at the double doors coming into the sanctuary. I saw (in the spirit with the eyes of my heart) Jesus walk in through the back door. He walked up and down the rows, looking into the faces of the people. He got to my row. He saw me, waved and said, "Hi, Regina."

"What are you doing here, Jesus?" I asked.

(Strange question, I know, when we are there to worship Him.)

"I decided to come by and see if anyone noticed I was here," He said.

He looked up and down each row, looking at the faces of the worshippers. He walked back by my row, waved again and walked out the back door. The seer gift gave me the ability to picture what was going on in the realm of the spirit.

Right after this experience, I was having a conversation with a pastor. I was sharing my heart about hearing from God. I told him that if I didn't hear God's voice every day, I felt the need to repent of not positioning myself and my heart to hear Him. The pastor said in essence, "Are you kidding me? I haven't heard His voice for at least a month."

My question to this pastor would be: "How do you speak for God if you haven't heard Him speak to you? How do you give the Word of the Lord if you haven't heard that Word from heaven?"

Some would say that it is not necessary to hear, see, or move by the Spirit because we have the Word. But if the Word is living and active, it will speak to us, giving us wisdom and input from Holy Spirit. Holy Spirit's purpose is to make the Father's will known to us and through us. Does God speak today? Is it only through the historical aspect of the Bible, like reading a history book to gain natural knowledge? Because I and others have experienced God's voice speaking directly to us through His Word, we know the Word is alive. The Word without the Spirit is similar to speaking the Truth without love. Rules without relationship can become abusive leadership. God is relational. He desired relationship when He created man. I love hearing my Father's voice through His Word anointed by His Spirit.

I am passionate for the voice of God to be heard; I am longing for God's people to see and hear by the Spirit. The seer gift opens up the realm of the Spirit revealing pictures, visions, and glimpses of another dimension.

I DECREE OVER YOU:

"There is a spirit realm. The Bible tells us that the eyes of our heart will be enlightened. I break the power of every false word that has been spoken over you and to you that negates the power of your spirit to see, hear, and live by the revelation of the spirit realm. I break the power of false doctrine of men who decree the power of God is no longer accessed or received in this realm. We are spirit beings, who live in a body, who operate in this realm by the power of our minds, will, and emotion, but possess the ability to live and move and have our being in the Lord."

ACTIVATION

Lord,

I repent for believing that you don't talk to your people anymore. I open my spiritual senses to see, hear, and perceive your voice. Forgive me for trusting in the voice of tradition and unbelieving religious entities instead of you. Speak to me in ways that will give me understanding and revelation that the voice I hear is you. I know you will never contradict yourself, and what you say will reflect your love for me. You are not a condemning God, but a rescuing Savior. Teach my spirit to listen with the ears of my heart and to see with the eyes of my heart. Forgive me for closing the door to your voice because I believed it wasn't possible to hear from you. You are the God of the possible. The Spirit realm is real, and I chose to enter into that reality through Jesus Christ who is the door. Awaken my Spirit to hear from heaven.

Amen.

6

What Will Be, Will Be?

Or What You See, You Decree?

The king said to Daniel, "Surely your God is the God of gods and the Lord of kings and a revealer of mysteries, for you were able to reveal this mystery."

Daniel 2:47

SEEING THE UNSEEN REALM OF THE SPIRIT reveals what has been hidden from the natural man. It answers unanswered questions: "Why is this happening to me" "Why is this not happening to me?"

It unlocks closed doors of opportunity, blessing, healing, provision, breakthrough, and a plethora of other benefits.

The Seer Gift

(I love that word, *plethora*. It can be used by fledging writers who want to sound intelligent or have run out of good ol' southwest Missouri words. But hopefully, you get the...picture.)

It also unlocks insight into roots of sickness, reveals pictures of things to come, prayer insights for people, states, territories, and nations. God loves seekers. He reveals secrets to His friends, as He did with Abraham.

Do you remember that old song, *Whatever Will Be, Will Be, Que Será, Será?* For those who aren't familiar with it, I have inserted it below. Before you read it, I have to tell you my opinion. I don't like it; it is a false narrative.

Que Será, Será

*When I was just a little girl
I asked my mother, "What will I be?"
"Will I be pretty, will I be rich?"
Here's what she said to me*

*"Que será, será
Whatever will be, will be
The future's not ours to see
Que será, será
What will be, will be"*

*When I grew up and fell in love
I asked my sweetheart what lies ahead
Will we have rainbows, day after day?
Here's what my sweetheart said:*

*"Que será, será
Whatever will be, will be
The future's not ours to see*

What Will Be, Will Be?

> *Que será, será*
> *What will be, will be"*
>
> *Now I have children of my own*
> *They ask their mother, "What will I be?"*
> *"Will I be handsome, will I be rich?"*
> *I tell them tenderly*
>
> *"Que será, será*
> *Whatever will be, will be*
> *The future's not ours to see*
> *Que será, será*
> *What will be, will be"*
>
> Jay Livingston/Ray Evans

I can't agree with the narrative of this song. It does not line up with the Word of God. Why pray if "whatever will be, will be"? We are called to be a participant on the earth. In agreement with God and His Word, we bring forth God's will through our intercession, through glimpses into the fourth dimension that give us direction, insight, and understanding. This song was very popular in its day. (I know—you are under 55 years old and you've never heard of it, but the belief system it portrays negates the power of prayer and decree from the Word of God.)

Let's take a look at Isaiah 46:9-10 (NASB).

> *Remember the former things long past, for I am God, and there is no other; I am God, and there is no one like Me, declaring the end from the beginning, and from ancient times, things which have not been done. Saying, 'My plan will be established, and I will accomplish all My good pleasure.'*

God knows the end from the beginning, and He is willing to share portions of the future with His friends who are seeking Him. Why would He do that? I believe He wants His people prepared for future events. He desires that we receive revelation of the future for the purpose of intercession that can stop the enemy's plans of destruction. Below is an example.

I took a team to Egypt in 2006. One of our intercessors in the states called us in Egypt to warn us about a possible attack. She said she had a vision of men with guns chasing us and that the Lord said we were not to get out of the car. That's all she told us. Here is the story of what happened.

The Lord sent us on an assignment to establish an altar of worship in the center of Egypt out of Isaiah 19. We did not go to Egypt without an assignment from the Lord that was confirmed many times. We knew we were sent for the Lord's purposes with specific instructions from Holy Spirit. The Lord kept us safe because we were in His will and walking in obedience to instructions He had given. We do not go into a volatile situation without apostolic alignment, assignment from heaven, and intercessors praying for the team.

We rented a car at the border between Israel and Egypt at the Taba gate. We loaded the team of five in the vehicle and began our jaunt across the Sinai Desert. Our goal was to reach Cairo before dark and find our accommodations. After about an hour of travel, still daylight, we noticed a vehicle following us through the desert. Suddenly, our driver stopped at an Egyptian checkpoint. Men with guns came running out toward us from the checkpoint. We were not sure what was going on. At that point, we stayed in the car. But curious me jumped out of the car to see what was going on. I did not remember the intercessor's vision about "not getting out of the car" because, in the heat of the moment, that insight was off my radar. When I saw the conflict between the Egyptian guards and the potential kidnappers, I quickly got back into the car. The guards at the checkpoint ran to the vehicle behind us and arrested the occupants, who had plans to capture Americans and hold them hostage. We were those "Americans." The Lord knew the end from the beginning and gave a vision to an intercessor to keep us safe. I learned an important lesson during this life-or-death situation to listen to those who see and hear in the Spirit.

Because we had insight from the spirit realm through the intercessor, whatever will be, did *not* be! Instead, we were saved. (Excuse the stilted wording. I'm trying to make a point.)

SEER EXPERIENCE

That intercessor gave us a warning from the Spirit of God from the seer realm. The seer gift is given by the Lord, accessed in our relationship with Holy Spirit. The "eyes of the heart" can be opened. Our intercessory friend seeing on the redeemed, cleansed lens of the heart, gave insight into a potential life-threatening situation.

(Hey, I'm on a roll here, so let me continue this downhill slide into pet peeves.)

When I hear a Christian say, "Everything happens for a reason."

Or I hear someone say, "It is what it is!" I cringe! Cringe description:

"When you cringe, your body language shows you don't like what you see and hear. You close your eyes and grimace. You may even jerk your body away from the offensive sight or sound, like the old picture of you in an "awkward stage" that makes you cringe whenever you see it."

Vocabulary.com

When I cringe, I close my eyes, jerk my body away, and walk away from that person quickly so I don't make the mistake of reacting to what I feel is skewed non-biblical thinking. Yes, God uses everything, but the meat of their statement comes from a misunderstanding of spiritual things.

If everything happens for a reason, what is that reason? If we aren't in relationship with the Spirit of God, we have to lean on our own understanding.

Trust in the Lord with all your heart; do not depend on your own understanding. Seek his will in all you do, and he will show you which path to take.

Proverbs 3:5-6 NLT

Reasonings, figuring it out, logical conclusions, can cut us off from the life flow of the Spirit of God. Seeking the Lord for the answer is a whole lot more accurate than the reasonings of man.

- What is the reason young men die on the battlefield?
- What is the reason babies die?

- What is the reason people go to drugs for solace?
- What is the reason children are abused or trafficked?
- What is the reason my mother died at a young age?

That "everything happens for a reason" statement is a shallow attempt to define God as aloof, distancing Himself from us and leaving us with "pie in the sky someday" understanding instead of pursuing God, using our spiritual gifts and our intimate relationship with Him to seek answers, roots, and revelation about misunderstood circumstances that appear to be out of our control.

> *And we know that God causes all things to work together for good to those who love God, to those who are called according to His purpose.*
>
> Romans 8:28 NASB

Romans 8:28 applies to those who love God and are called according to His purpose. It is not a general statement that covers every person on earth.

"It is, what it is." Really?

That statement comes from a victim mentality. I believe all things can be changed to line up with God's will On the earth. Accepting what is around us as if circumstances control our lives, is nonsense for the believer. I love the scripture in Psalm 115:16:

> *The highest heavens belong to the LORD, but the earth he has given to mankind.*

Each time I read that scripture, I remember an old television show where the main character was a spy. He was given assignments he could chose to take or reject. He always got his assignments in an old phone booth. He would wait for the phone to ring, answer it and listen to his next assignment. The voice on the line would say to him, "Your assignment, if you choose to take it, is…."

I don't recall that he ever refused to take the assignment he was given.

I hear the Lord speaking right now, not from an old phone booth, but from the spirit into the ears of my heart.

I have given you the assignment of the earth. You can take that assignment or be relegated to a wrong belief system of "whatever will be, will be" or you can blame Me (God) for all your troubles. You guys on the earth keep saying I am in control. Hey, I'm not a controlling God. I AM in charge, but I have assigned the earth to you. Would you please quit blaming me for your troubles? I have given you authority. Now use it!

Declare my Word, listen to my voice. A lot of what you are experiencing, you could have avoided if you knew the power of my Spirit and walked in that power. I'm not saying this to condemn you. I am saying it to motivate you to decree my Word into your world. Your assignment if you choose to take it is the earth. If you don't take your place, your assignment, I Am seen as the "bad God," because I didn't come through for you.

I am not into witchcraft. I didn't make people as robots. I gave them free will. They can choose to do what they want. But your prayers and decrees release angelic forces on your behalf and can change the course of your future.

Call on me and I will answer you and tell you great and mighty things which you do not know (Jeremiah 33:3 NKJV)

(In essence, God was saying, "I will even give you my phone number!")

The earth is groaning for the manifestation of the Sons of God. I have called you to the Kingdom for such a time as this."

> *I consider that our present sufferings are not comparable to the glory that will be revealed in us. The creation waits in eager expectation for the revelation of the sons of God. For the creation was subjected to futility, not by its own will, but because of the One who subjected it, in hope that the creation itself will be set free from its bondage to decay and brought into the glorious freedom of the children of God.*
>
> *We know that the whole creation has been groaning together in the pains of childbirth until the present time. Not only that, but we ourselves, who have the first fruits of the Spirit, groan inwardly as we wait eagerly for our adoption as sons, the redemption of our bodies. For in this hope, we were saved; but hope that is seen is no hope at all. Who hopes for what he can already see? But if we hope for what we do not yet see, we wait for it patiently.*
>
> Romans 8:18-25

MOTIVATION

Pursue love, yet desire earnestly spiritual gifts, but especially that you may prophesy.

I Corinthians 14:1 NASB

Functioning in the seer gift opens up the spiritual realm to one of the five senses available to every Spirit-led believer. We are born with five senses in the natural: sight, smell, touch, hearing, and taste. These are available spiritually as well. But they must be accessed, activated, cultivated, and used for Kingdom purposes. We know that gifts are not to be demonstrated for personal gain but are to be used to benefit others. When I first became acquainted with spiritual gifts years ago, I was afraid to allow them to be seen. The fear of rebuke, the fear of man, and the fear of being wrong caused me to hesitate. One of the earliest examples of this struggle brought me to the place of obedience.

The Holy Spirit had given me a word for someone in the audience of a Christian gathering. I did not know the identity of that person, nor did I want to be obedient to the Spirit. I was afraid to risk being wrong in front of all those people. The Lord spoke to my heart and said, "That word I gave isn't for you. It's for one of my children who is struggling. Be obedient!"

I could picture a struggling person with the eyes of my heart. I had to decide if I was going to let my fear rule or my God rule. I got out of my chair, walked to the front with trembling lips and weak knees. I found the person in authority and told him meekly that I felt I had a word for someone in the audience. There was a part of me that was hoping he would say, "Go sit down." But he didn't. He actually handed me the microphone. The Lord wanted His Word given to someone whom He loved dearly. I had to be obedient.

My voice quivered as I spoke:

There is someone here who was given up for adoption by your biological parents. You have felt rejected, unloved, and left out all of your life. Even though you have adoptive parents, your heart hurts from rejection. The Lord wants you to know He has chosen you to be His child. He is your father, and He wrote the plan for your life. You were not an accident. He wants you to know how much He loves you and is reaching out to you this evening with this word for you. He has a purpose for your life.

I returned to my seat as quickly as possible, hoping I was not out of order or just plain wrong. After the meeting, a man came to me with tears in his eyes, thanking me for that word. He said it was for him. He had come to the church looking for some sign, some word for him personally, that proved God's love for him. The man had planned to commit suicide if he did not hear that his life had purpose. He thought he was an accident, but God intervened by His grace through the word He had given me.

What a shock to me! My obedience to the voice of the Lord to share this word in a public setting saved a life!! I was overwhelmed, emotional, and majorly impacted by the results of obedience to the Spirit of God. So, what would have happened if I hadn't been obedient to release the word? Perhaps the Lord would have prompted someone else to intervene in this man's life. Perhaps a man, with a destiny yet unfulfilled, could have carried out his plan to destroy himself. This was a major life lesson for me! It continues to, press me forward out of myself and into obedience to give out what the Lord has given me.

Yes, the Lord gives gifts to us for our stewardship. They don't belong to us, but we operate in them to benefit and advance His kingdom. In a sense, they are the "keys to the Kingdom" that Jesus said He was giving to us in Matthew 16:19. "I will give you the keys to the kingdom of heaven;" Keys unlock realms previously unseen, revelation previously unknown, and freedom previously inaccessible.

Have you ever tried to unlock your vehicle from across a parking lot, so you could find it? I love my electronic key. When I click it, the taillights of my car light up, and if I click it again, my horn makes a noise, directing me to the place where I parked it. Keys can give direction to things that have been lost, visions that have been left on a parking lot, things you were going to get back to, but took another route instead.

DECREE

I decree over you that you will find what you have left behind. The dreams you have left parked on the back parking lot of your memories will be accessed again. Abandoned dreams, abandoned visions, lost potential are waiting for you to press the key of hope, find where you parked them, open the door and get in the driver's seat again. It's not too late. That lost key is being found today.

A vision is a picture of the purpose or will of God released into the earth.

Seer Experience

It was Sunday morning. In the natural realm, I was seated in a chair surrounded by other church-goers. We were in the midst of the message when suddenly I was pulled up into a vision. In this vision, I was in the heavenlies, standing in a long line of priests who were dressed alike. They were wearing white robes, had crowns on their heads, sashes around their waists, breastplates covering their chests, and sandals on their feet. They each were carrying a gift on a beautiful gold pillow to give to the King. The line was long, and I was standing a long way from the throne waiting my turn to present a gift. Suddenly, I realized I had no pillow, nor did I have a gift to present to the King. At this realization, I became overwhelmed with grief, realizing my hands were empty. As I was weeping from the lack of a suitable gift, Jesus appeared to me in the line.

"Regina, all I want is for you to give back to me the gifts I have given to you."

Then He opened up my abdomen and pulled out the gifts He had given me. (*Stay with me here.*)

He spoke again: "Use these for my glory and the advancement of my Kingdom. You can only give back to me the things I have given you."

He pulled out of me dreams that I had long forgotten. He pulled out desires I had given up on.

Suddenly, I was back in my seat in the Sunday morning service. Needless to say, my focus was not on what was being said in front of me by the speaker. I was focused on the experience that had impacted me beyond words. I remembered the parable of the talents that Jesus spoke about in in Matthew 25. I realized that the parable applied to me in a way I hadn't perceived until this moment. I had buried within myself talents that had been given to me by the Lord.

Among other gifts was an unmined gift of writing. The Lord had called me to be a writer. I had written three books but had put the gift on hold, believing I did not have time to focus on it and was not gifted to do it. In that vision, I repented to the Lord for my procrastination and asked Him to pull it out of me so I could multiply the talent He had given to me. This is one of the books I had buried within me.

Thinking of the parable of the buried talents, are we not made of soil? Are not the gifts within us the talents He has given to use for His glory?

As I read this parable again, I put myself in the picture. I had buried gifts within myself in the soil of my vessel. I repented that day for burying them, pulled them out, and activated them within me by the power of the Spirit. I knew the Lord expected me and others to multiply our gifts by using them. We can bury them for safekeeping, hide them from others for many reasons, or use them for His purposes. Opening up our gifts, using them to advance the Kingdom of God in our lives and the lives of others is crucial to the advancement of the body of Christ.

Our motivation for activating the gifts within us is first of all obedience to the Lord, but also for the purpose of ministering to people.

So, how did I "see" that vision. It's almost like daydreaming. All of us have had that experience. Most of us were reprimanded for it—especially by schoolteachers trying to keep our attention. I remember sitting in school on a warm spring day, looking out the window at the playground. Suddenly, in my heart (my imagination) I was there on the playground. I was swinging. My feet were reaching the sky. A bird flew by. A butterfly was warming itself in the sun, sitting on a flower. I wasn't in school anymore. I was touching the sky with my heart. I was feeling the thrill of being outside on a warm spring day. The voice of the teacher was drowned out by the sounds of nature around me.

Suddenly, I heard my name called!

"Regina!! I just asked you a question," she demanded. "You had better quit daydreaming. I don't know where you were, but I spoke to you several times before you heard me."

I think I had to stay after school or write 100 times, "I will not daydream in school!" (It was worth it.)

Daydreaming is similar to the seer gift. I wasn't on the school playground. I wasn't swinging. There was no bird flying by, nor was there a butterfly warming itself on a nearby flower. I saw myself there. I pictured where I wanted to be. This was an inner desire that I tried to make a reality. It was not led by the Spirit of God, but by my own volition. But it illustrates the ability to picture another reality. Daydreaming is not a bad thing. (Of course, it depends on where you are when it happens.) It actually accesses our ability to see or picture things. We have the ability to see with the eyes of our hearts. When this is accessed and activated by the Spirit of God, it can be developed into a seer gift that helps others and releases God's input into our realm.

ACTIVATION

> *But blessed are your eyes, because they see; and your ears, because they hear. For truly I say to you that many prophets and righteous men desired to see what you see, and did not see it, and to hear what you hear, and did not hear it.*
>
> Matthew 13:16-17 NASB

Lord,

I ask you to activate the seer gift within me by the power of your Spirit. May I see what you see and hear what you are saying so I can implement heaven's purposes into the earth to bless and motivate your children toward victory. In the name of Jesus, by the power of Holy Spirit.

Amen.

7

🗝 The Power of Courage

THE BOOK OF ESTHER IS an accurate description of decrees. When we read about Haman and his devious manipulation that culminated in an evil decree against the Jews, we see the power of a king's decree. This is the evil decree that Haman talked King Xerxes into releasing.

> Then Haman said to King Xerxes, "There is a certain people dispersed among the peoples in all the provinces of your kingdom who keep themselves separate. Their customs are different from those of all other people, and they do not obey the king's laws; it is not in the king's best interest to tolerate them. If it pleases the king, let a decree be issued to destroy them, and I will give ten thousand talents of silver to the king's administrators for the royal treasury."
> So the king took his signet ring from his finger and gave it to Haman son of Hammedatha, the

> *Agagite, the enemy of the Jews. "Keep the money," the king said to Haman, "and do with the people as you please."*
>
> Esther 3:8-11

This is no doubt a familiar story to those who attended Sunday school. Esther has become a heroine for Christian girls as she demonstrated fearlessness in the face of potential death not only for her people, the Jews, but also for herself. Without the king's scepter extended to her as she entered his court, she could have been immediately condemned to death. Esther was brave enough to petition the king for a reversal of the evil decree against her people.

But the king could not reverse what he had previously written and sealed with his signet ring. He replied to Esther.

> *Now write another decree in the king's name in behalf of the Jews as seems best to you, and seal it with the king's signet ring—for no document written in the king's name and sealed with his ring can be revoked.*
>
> Esther 8:8

The new decree did not negate the first one, but gave the people warning and the release to defend themselves from attack. The Jews indeed fought back and won against their enemies.

> *The Jews struck down all their enemies with the sword, killing and destroying them, and they did what they pleased to those who hated them.*
>
> Esther 9:5

The Power of Courage

People with courage do things that require conquering fear, e.g., fear of being wrong, fear of man, fear of reprisal, or fear of death. Esther had courage to enter a room, the throne room of the king. This was forbidden without an invitation. She faced her fear, conquered it, and walked out with an obedient heart the instructions she had been given by her Uncle Mordecai.

I believe he is a picture of Holy Spirit, who gives us instruction as well.

I had been aware of the story of Irena Sendler. A documentary about World War 2 included portions of her bravery, but sadly I had forgotten her name. I forgot her, but the Lord did not forget, nor does He forget our labor of love and obedience to His voice.

Irena's story is a story of courage. "There are endless examples of courage buried in the ruins of the Holocaust, but Irena Sendler's story stands out. When the Nazis invaded her native Poland and rounded up all the Jews into a walled-in ghetto, Sendler knew what was going to happen. She was a social worker and got credentials as a nurse so she could sneak food and medicine into the ghetto. What she snuck out was even more phenomenal: It's estimated that Sendler and her group helped get approximately 2500 children out of the ghetto—sedated and placed in the bottom of toolboxes or lying in burlap sacks at the bottom of her truck—and sent them through a network of like-minded comrades to Christian orphanages, where they were given new identities. She kept their real names in a jar buried in her backyard. Sendler was eventually caught by the Nazis, who imprisoned and tortured her, breaking both of her legs.

When the war ended, she devoted herself to reuniting children with their families, though it proved nearly impossible to do so."

Courage in the face of fear develops an obedient heart. Fear paralyzes; obedience motivates. Decisions motivated by fear cause silence in the face of opportunity. Decisions motivated by obedience empower the voice to speak up, producing opportunities to bring change into debilitating circumstances.

ACTIVATION

Lord,

Give me the courage to step out in faith when you release your Word to me. Help me trust in your input in my life. Help me respond to you, being a good steward of what you release to me. Forgive me for being unwilling to risk the obedience you desired in me.

Amen.

BUILDING THE KINGDOM

Several years ago, the Lord directed me to purchase a building that we had been renting to house a food pantry. We had been renting it for several months, when the owner of the building and a realtor who was trying to sell the building came to me and said,

"Are you going to purchase this building? Because if you are not, we are going to kick you out of it. We don't care if you are a food pantry. We need to sell this building. Are you going to buy it?"

I knew the Lord had said that the building was mine. In the face of their intimidation, I said, "Yes, I am buying this building."

They told me the price. I had no down payment, nor did I have funds for closing costs, etc. My mind was racing, and my heart was beating when I made that commitment. After they left, I ran to the Lord. I knew He had said the building was mine but, when I looked at the circumstances, they weren't lining up with the word the Lord had given me. A ministry friend of mine wrote letters to a few of our colleagues. We got some support and started a fund for the down payment. A local bank had agreed to loan us the money after we had secured the funds. We were $6,000 short of the down payment when the banker called.

"Are you going to be able to sign the papers tomorrow? Do you have all of your down payment?"

I looked into my heart. I did not have what the Lord said I was going to have at that moment. I stepped out in faith. (Faith is risky.)

"Yes, I will have the money tomorrow, and we will purchase the building."

The closing on the building was scheduled. The only thing missing was $6,000. I prayed a desperate prayer. I was walking on water and just knew I was going to sink. Was I going to believe the Lord or look at circumstances? It was time to go visit our son and his wife and our two grandchildren. I wasn't sure if I could enjoy that visit because of the pressure I was under. We were traveling in our car when the Lord spoke to me.

He said, "Go through your phone contacts. One will jump out at you. Call them and they will provide the rest of the funds you need for the down payment tomorrow."

Suddenly, courage rose up in me, and I started looking through my contacts. One did jump out at me. It was halfway through my list of contacts, so it took some time. I worked up the courage to call them.

"Hi! This is Regina. I am purchasing a building to house our food pantry. We feed the poor in our city. We have been renting it but have signed a contract to purchase it. We are short $6,000. Would you and your husband be willing to loan us the money for three months? I believe we can pay it back by then."

She yelled at her husband to ask him if they could do that. Meanwhile, I was trembling with fear and wondering how I had gotten myself in this predicament.

I heard him respond, "When does she need it?"

She asked me, "When do you need it?"

"Tomorrow," I said.

I heard him yell again, "Well, it's just sitting there in the bank. We can do that. Where do we need to send it?"

I remember getting off of the phone with tears in my eyes, wondering why God required that kind of stupidity out of me. Or was it faith? You will have to decide for yourself. The end result was that we purchased that building and it is now fully paid for. It required faith and courage to step out on a limb (or was it walking on water like Peter did), to be obedient. The Lord makes a way where there is no way. We have since purchased another building for a different ministry we oversee. The Lord again provided the funds we needed to complete the purchase. I do not counsel others to do this, unless you know that you know the Lord is leading you. But when you are sure of His leading, obedience is your only option. Courage in the face of adverse circumstances develops within us and gives us confidence to obey the voice of the Lord.

8

The Kingdom

The Domain and Reign of The King

THE SEER GIFT GIVES ACCESS to the mysteries of God. What is a mystery? *Yourdictionary.com* defines mystery as: "something that is secret, something where there is no clear explanation, something difficult to understand or explain…"

Jesus said in Matthew 16:19 ESV:

> *I will give you the keys of the kingdom of heaven; and whatever you bind on earth shall be bound in heaven, and whatever you loose on earth shall be loosed in heaven.*

The seer gift accesses keys to release the kingdom, the domain of the King, in people, land, and territories. It allows us to access undisclosed wisdom for perplexing problems. Since our God is all-knowing, we can find answers from another realm that open doors in the natural realm previously shut.

> *Yet we do speak wisdom among those who are mature; a wisdom, however, not of this age nor of the rulers of this age, who are passing away; but we speak God's wisdom in a mystery, the hidden wisdom which God predestined before the ages to our glory; the wisdom which none of the rulers of this age has understood; for if they had understood it they would not have crucified the Lord of glory; but just as it is written, "THINGS WHICH EYE HAS NOT SEEN AND EAR HAS NOT HEARD, AND WHICH HAVE NOT ENTERED THE HEART OF MAN, ALL THAT GOD HAS PREPARED FOR THOSE WHO LOVE HIM." For to us God revealed them through the Spirit; for the Spirit searches all things, even the depths of God."*
>
> 1 Corinthians 2:6-10 NASB

Spiritual gifts are accessed internally by the input of Holy Spirit. They are revealed by the Spirit of God within us. When we are born of the Spirit by the act of salvation, we position ourselves to move in the gifts of the Spirit. The baptism of the Spirit immerses us, activating those gifts. They can remain dormant within us if we do not walk in obedience to the Spirit's promptings or if we have not accessed the gifts because of false information that denies their existence.

I remember sitting as a student in a class on the Book of Acts in a Christian Bible College. The professor said to the students, "if you don't remember anything else about this class, remember this, the gifts of the spirit passed away with the apostles and disciples of Jesus. We now have the Word of God, and we don't need the gifts of the Spirit anymore."

At that time in my life, I didn't doubt the professor's words. For most of my life, I had been taught against the supernatural move of God in the denominational church we attended. I heard the words of those who were more intelligent than I and took them at their word. Just one problem…they were wrong.

A.W. Tozer says it this way,

> The truth is, God never thought of his church apart from the Holy Spirit. We were born of the Spirit. We are baptized into the body of Christ by the Spirit. We are anointed with the Spirit. We are led by the Spirit. We are taught by the Spirit, and the Spirit is the medium, the Divine solution, in which God holds His church. The hymnist portrayed the Holy Spirit as the "essence of the godhead uncreated.
>
> God never dreamed of His people apart from the Holy Spirit, and accordingly made promises to them."

(Tozer: Mystery of the Holy Spirit, pg. 15-16)

The empowering of the Spirit of God must be restored to the body of Christ. Without the fruits of the Spirit and the gifts of the Spirit, we are left to our own "good" works. I love that old song,

Spirit of the Living God
Fall afresh on me.
Melt me, mold me
Fill me, use me.
Spirit of the Living God
Fall afresh on me.

My prayer for all of us is that we become empowered by the Spirit of God, lay down our self-efforts, depend on the power of the cross of Jesus that brought us back into relationship with God, and receive the power of the third member of the Godhead, the Spirit of God Himself. I have seen His power and cannot deny His miraculous power to save, deliver, heal, transform, and reveal Himself to us and through us.

ACTIVATION

Lord,

I choose to read this scripture with an innocent heart that has not been tainted by those who have cut and pasted the Bible to suit their personal deceptions or denominational affiliations. The gifts were released after the Lord's ascension. I will not negate these gifts by wrong thinking patterns. I choose to receive, activate, and use the seer gift to mature the body of Christ and open up answers for those who are sitting in darkness. I chose not to ignore lightning flashes of revelation that Holy Spirit is releasing to me for the help of others. The eyes of my heart have been enlightened by the Spirit of God within me. I am a believer; I believe you Lord that you want to use me as your vessel with the ability to see spiritually for the

The Kingdom

purpose of assisting your people on their journey to Christlikeness.

Amen.

PICTURING THE PROCESS

I was a student in the third grade. We were learning our multiplication tables. Mrs. Whitesell had written them on the chalkboard. (I know! I know! This story has to be old because they don't use chalkboards anymore. Now it's whiteboards, computers, I-pads etc. You are so keen in your perception! Now let's get back to our story.)

My desk was situated in the back row. I was unable to see the board, let alone the multiplication tables written on it. I was not aware that I could not see. I thought everyone saw things as I did, blurry and unclear. I also thought I was incapable of learning these challenging math principles. (Don't forget, I was eight years old. I don't want to put myself down too much.)

A couple of weeks later, the school did eye tests to see if any students needed glasses. It was revealed that I could not see very well. My parents took me to an eye doctor, and after an eye test, glasses were prescribed. The world suddenly cleared up. I could see what I could not see previously. Multiplication tables were easy after that. I was now capable of conquering those tables. Just ask me any of them now, and I can tell you without using my calculator.

My journey to revelation concerning the seer gift had begun. I wore glasses for many years, changing styles, and at the same time increasing lens strength. My engagement picture reminds me of those years. I wore the cat glasses. Remember those? Well, maybe not. But ask your mother or grandmother; she will remember. We all wore them back then. They were in style.

I now see these changes as prophetic for the hardness of my religious heart. You see, I grew up in a denomination that taught the gifts of the Spirit "passed away" with the disciples. We, of course, thought we were right. Later, I understood that we did not believe in the gifts because we had not experienced them for ourselves. We had not seen them demonstrated, nor did we believe they were genuine. It's easy to dismiss something as non-existent rather than break out of the bondage of false religious concepts. Remember, I couldn't see what was right in front of me, naturally as well as spiritually.

Later, I discovered that LASIK surgery was available, and I could have my eyes fixed to see without thick glasses. I scheduled surgery with an eye doctor, who happened to be Jewish. I remember going into surgery wide awake, being positioned on a table under a huge machine with a laser that would burn and reshape the cornea of each eye. The doctor had to create a thin hinged corneal flap, pulling it back to expose the corneal tissue. After reshaping the cornea, actually using a laser to correct a refractive error, the doctor replaced the flap. Immediately after the procedure, I could see without glasses. My cornea had been reshaped.

I can see the prophetic symbolism in this surgery. My eyes were reshaped. I saw what I couldn't see before that surgery. My perception about seeing had also been reshaped; I could see clearly, without glasses, what had been blurry previously. I traded my thick glasses for no glasses at all. That Jewish doctor in the natural realm represents Jesus. He is ready to do LASIK surgery on us, reshaping our visionary capability to see clearly what appeared to be blurry or non-existent previously.

I hope you aren't tired of this story, because it culminates in a final surgery to remove cataracts from my eyes. Prophetically I believe cataracts represent a world view that accumulates across our vision screen, making it difficult to perceive the world around us clearly. It eventually leads to complete blindness.

I had cataracts removed from both eyes. After that surgery, I was angry. My vision was so full of light that I thought the doctor had taken all the color out of my vision. Previous to the surgery, everything in my vision had a yellowish cast to it. When that was removed by surgery, I reacted thinking there was too much light and not enough color (yellow) in my vision. I realized later as I adapted to this new clear vision, that what was perceived as normal was actually colored by the cataracts.

I can see the prophetic symbolism in this as well. I believe the spirit of this world is similar to cataracts.

> *And even if our gospel is veiled, it is veiled to those who are perishing, in whose case the god of this world has blinded the minds of the unbelieving so that they might not see the light of the gospel of the glory of Christ, who is the image of God.*
>
> 2 Corinthians 4:3-4 NASB

I am called to be a seer; the Lord has given me that gift, but it was not developed overnight. My journey into spiritual sight mirrored my physical journey. I wanted my natural eyes to see, and I asked the Lord to open the eyes of my heart. He performed both of those miracles. The natural miracle came from skilled physicians; the spiritual came through the Great Physician.

ACTIVATION

Lord,

I ask that you do whatever spiritual surgery is necessary to open the eyes of my heart. Where my perceptions are blurry because of false teaching or unbelief, I give you permission as the Great Physician to increase my vision to see as you see. Thank you that it is your desire to increase my ability to accept, perceive, receive, and unpack spiritual vision. Whether it is flashes of light from the spiritual realm, dreams, or visions, I ask you, my Jewish doctor, to reshape my vision, and remove the cataracts of worldly perspectives from my vision.

Amen.

RECEIVE

Scenes that flash into our minds from the spiritual realm that reveal a picture to the eyes of your heart can be the beginning of developing a seer gift. Many of us have "seen" these brief pictures, but perhaps dismissed them as unimportant. Another issue that can negate these pictures from being received is experience that denies access to daydreaming. You remember sitting in a boring classroom, fading out into a field of flowers, trees, birds, waterfalls, and picnics. You could see yourself there, enjoying your perceived surroundings, when you heard the voice of your teacher calling you back to the reality of the classroom. These "daydreams" are the place where the seer gift is developed. Unknowingly, the teacher instructed you to deny yourself the opportunity to see with the eyes of your heart. Your heart wasn't into the boring environment, so you created your own environment with the eyes of your heart.

The Lord uses that ability within you to give you pictures from the realm of the Spirit. Your heart can see. Receiving that possibility is key to unlocking the seer realm.

Here is an example: The Lord had given me an assignment to take a team to Romania. Prior to going, I was in prayer for the people of that land. I began to see them with the eyes of my heart. I guess you could say I was "daydreaming" about them. At one point during our trip to Romania, I suddenly realized I was sitting in the midst of the people the Lord had shown me during my preparation prayer prior to leaving the U.S. I envisioned them with the eyes of my heart before I saw them with my natural eyes. The seer gift activated within me allowing me to see the people we were going to meet prior to actually meeting them in person.

9

🗝 Ascendancy of the Spirit

ONE OF THE DEFINITIONS OF ASCENDANCY is occupation of position of dominant power or influence. After our salvation experience, our spirit man comes alive; we are born again. That means Jesus is Savior, but it is a process to make Him Lord of our thoughts, our actions, and our motivations. It is a process of gradual submission of our will to the will of the Lord. When Jesus prayed, "not my will but Thine be done" in the garden of Gethsemane, it was a real struggle that brought Jesus to genuine agony of soul. He was facing the cross, the pain, and the burden of the sins of all mankind. Yes, this God/man struggled with His flesh to the point of sweating blood. It is a battle to let go and trust the Lord with the things most precious to us. It is a process of building trust in His goodness and placing our lives in His hands without restraint.

Recently, our prayer team had the privilege of praying for a young man who was desperate to restore his marriage. When he came into our office, he sat down and began to tell us what he wanted God to do for him. Some of that is understandable, but when he wouldn't slow down long enough for us to dialog, we knew his soul was in superman mode. He was going to get this done and God was going to do it his way. It was as if God was his servant, and the young man was telling the Lord what to do and giving suggestions on how it could be carried out. There was little understanding of the Lordship of Jesus in his life, although the young man was born again and in ministry. He was so afraid of losing his wife that he had been stalking her.

Fear is a motivating factor in allowing the soul to take over. As new believers, our trust in the Lord has to grow. As God demonstrates His faithfulness to us, and our trust in Him grows, we can let go of our agendas, our strong will, and submit the situation to His complete oversight.

The young man had to let go of his agenda, dialog with the Lord, and turn his life and his marriage over to Jesus. In doing so, his pain and fear surfaced. We were able to help him move toward releasing his future and his marriage into God's capable hand.

Trusting God and letting go of our desire to control our lives is key to receiving insight and revelation from the realm of the spirit. If our soul is still orchestrating our lives and decisions, then it has not submitted to the direction and leading of the Spirit of God within.

It is difficult for many to actually submit their lives in entirety to the direction of God. I will never forget an experience I had with the Lord several years ago. I was notorious for "helping God out." As a new believer, recently filled with the Spirit, I wanted to introduce others to the power of God. I was in the midst of planning several gatherings and was asking God to bless them. They were, in my thinking, a great opportunity for God to show up and demonstrate His power to change lives. One day I was driving down the road in my car, thinking about the next gathering I was planning for God. Suddenly, the Lord spoke to me, "when are you going to stop building a stage for me to perform on? Who is the Lord and who is the servant?"

That question changed my life. He began to speak to me further.

"We are going to switch places. I want you to come to me and ask for my direction in your life. Each morning, show up at my doorstep in prayer and I will speak to you and tell you what to do."

He wasn't being dictatorial or harsh. I had it out of order. He was aligning me for greater things. If I'm in charge and He is my servant, we aren't going very far. I'm sure I would have laid exhausted on the floor in a week or so. I'm thankful the Lord rescued me from myself and my "good" ideas.

From that day forward, I laid my agenda for God in the dust and petitioned Him for fresh direction and insight from heaven. Until my plans were submitted to His plans, my spirit connected to God's Holy Spirit, He was not in control. My human spirit, the source of all my good ideas, was dominating over the spirit of the Lord within me.

Allowing the Spirit of God within us to lead is an ongoing process. I remember my mother calling me a strong-willed child. In other words, I wanted my way. Perhaps all children have a will that has to be yielded to parents, teachers, and earthly authorities, but as a teenager, I did not listen to authority. After I learned to drive, I was given use of one of the family cars. My dad told me that I could use the car, but I was not to go outside the city limits. Being strong-willed, you can guess what I did. I took the car outside the city limits and traveled to a neighboring city. It was a rude awakening when I looked in my rearview mirror and saw my parents following me. I knew I was in trouble. Grounded for a week was pretty minor considering my outright rebellion.

The Lord was faithful to hammer that rebellion out of me. It culminated in my encounter with Him as He gently asked me to change places allowing Him to be my Lord instead of my servant. Leadership is still in me, but it is now submitted to Holy Spirit. Don't get me wrong. I'm sure I'm still in process, as we all are.

Recently, we were praying for a young man. Let's call him George. (Not his real name, of course). The Lord led me to ask George if he had Jesus in his heart. He said that he did. I then told him to look inside his heart in the spirit realm and tell me where Jesus is sitting in his heart. He closed his eyes, looked with the eyes of his heart and told me Jesus was in there, but he had him held behind a door. Jesus was not on the throne of this man's heart yet.

"Can you let Him out from behind that door?" I asked.

"It is hard for me," George said. "I like to be in control."

"Are you willing?" I questioned.

"Yes, I am. I need to ask His forgiveness for not making Him Lord."

George prayed a very genuine prayer, releasing Jesus to not only be Savior, but also Lord.

"Where is Jesus now?" I asked. "Is He on the throne of your heart now?"

George closed his eyes, picturing with the eyes of his heart, where Jesus was sitting.

"He is on the Throne of my heart now."

We were blessed to see this transformation of George's heart. The Lord used the seer realm to show us the condition of the heart.

Until we take a subservient position in our relationship with God in which He is not only Savior but Lord, we will not be given greater stewardship of the mysteries of God.

As a parent, I understand this. My children learned to ride a tricycle, then a bicycle, then monitored drive time in the car. When they could be trusted with the motored vehicle, I released them with greater responsibility. It's not that they "earned" anything by their behavior; rather they demonstrated responsible stewardship over what had been released to them.

My children had responsibilities when they were growing up. I would give them instructions to clean their room, put the dishes in the dishwasher, sweep the floor, etc. Without fail, they would try to avoid obedience. They hoped I would forget about it and allow them to go outside and play or watch their favorite television program. I would hear them talking to each other.

"Let's ask mom if we can watch TV and then do our work."

They kept trying that trick, but I was onto them.

"No, I'm not telling you another thing until you get your jobs finished. No questions! No bargaining for privileges until you do what I said."

Our Father is a good parent. He releases to us direction, instruction, and vision. He fully expects us to obey His instructions, not as a demanding Father, but as a loving parent. He knows what is best for us and wants to use us to exhort, encourage, empower, and minister to others. When we don't listen and obey, the Lord has to speak to someone else who is obedient in order to release His words into the earth and into the hearts of those He loves.

There is another important issue here. I have discovered that disobedience clogs up our spiritual ears. It's as if I can hear the Lord saying, "I'm not giving you another instruction until you show yourself faithful."

> *The Lord God has given Me the tongue of disciples, so that I may know how to sustain the weary one with a word. He awakens Me morning by morning, He awakens My ear to listen as a disciple. The Lord God has opened My ear, And I was not disobedient, nor did I turn back.*
>
> Isaiah 50:4-5 NASB

It really goes back to being a faithful steward of what Holy Spirit has given to us. What is a steward? A steward is one who looks after another's property.

> *Who then is the faithful and wise servant, whom the master has put in charge of the servants in his household to give them their food at the proper time? It will be good for that servant whose master finds him doing so when he returns. Truly I tell you, he will put him in charge of all his possessions.*
>
> Matthew 24:45-47

I've heard many a frustrated person ask me this question: "Why doesn't God speak to me anymore? I used to hear Him, but now it's as if He isn't speaking or I'm not hearing. What is the problem?"

It's a simple answer. You didn't do the last thing He asked you to do. When we do not obey the voice of the Spirit of God, our ears become dull of hearing. Repentance is the key to open them up again. We simply ask forgiveness for disobedience responding to His promptings and ask the Lord to open the ears of our heart to hear again and the eyes of our heart to see again. I have seen this directive applied in several situations and the result is restoration of sight and sound in the Spirit realm. Repentance is not just saying, "I'm sorry." It is a change of heart and an exchange of our thoughts for the mind and character of Christ.

ACTIVATION

Lord,

Forgive me for my directive prayers. I have been telling you what to do for years, not realizing that I had not really submitted my life to your direction. Instead of talking to you and getting your direction, I have been telling you what to do. I have been building a stage for you to perform on. You are not my puppet; you are my Lord. I submit myself to your control, to your guidance, and to your leadership. I want to be led by your Spirit, not by my good ideas and scattered thoughts. I know that until I submit my heart completely to your leadership, my soul is still in control. I choose the ascendancy of the Spirit within me. I choose to allow you first place, dominance, in my choices. Guide me; I lay down my agendas and choose your leadership in my life. As you lead me, help me grow in my trust in your goodness and love. You want what is best for me.

Amen.

10

⚿ Servant or Son?

Identity

No longer do I call you servants, for a servant does not know what his master is doing, but I have called you friends, for all things that I heard from My Father, I have made known to you.

John 15:15

IN 2 KINGS 6, GOD OPENED THE EYES of Elijah's servant and blinded the eyes of the looters, scavengers.

Elisha was facing a group of looters, scavengers, Arameans who periodically came into the land of Israel to steal. Elisha continued to warn the King of Israel describing the exact places they were going to raid. The Arameans could not steal from Israel because of Elisha's warnings. The King of Aram was so angered by Elisha that he sent his men to Dothan, where Elisha was staying, to capture the prophet. He sent a strong force with horses and chariots to capture him.

The servant was fearful when he saw the evil forces surrounding them. All the servant could see was the natural army coming in full force to take them captive. He could not see spiritually. Elisha said in 2 Kings 6:16,

Don't be afraid, the prophet answered. Those who are with us are more than those who are with them.

The servant could not see in the spirit because of his identity as a servant. Elisha, who was a friend of God, had spiritual sight. The angel armies that were gathered all around them were not seen even though they were there. At that point, Elisha asked the Lord to open the eyes of his servant.

And Elisha prayed, "O Lord, open his eyes so he may see." Then the Lord opened the servant's eyes, and he looked and saw the hills full of horses and chariots of fire all around Elisha.

2 Kings 6:17

Knowing our identity as a son or daughter of God is crucial to "seeing in the Spirit." The Lord speaks to His friends, His sons and daughters. Identity is key to seeing with the eyes of our hearts.

Several years ago, I was standing at my kitchen sink, removing sticky labels from the bottom of glassware that we had purchased for our son's wedding. There were 99 Libby water glasses, and each had a sticky label. I was well into this process when the Lord spoke to me and said, "I have called you to take labels off of my people."

Labels tell us what we are looking at. I recently bought a pair of jeans. The label told me the brand, the size, instructions for washing, and the price. My jeans had an accurate label. What was written on them described them well. But there are times that we live our whole lives with an inaccurate label. Believe me, I understand living with a label that was put on me through circumstances but did not line up with the Word of God.

The next Sunday, I was speaking at a local church. I kept being drawn to a young lady on the back row. I knew the Lord was pointing her out to me. I interrupted my message to address her.

"Young lady on the back row, what is your name?"

She stood up and timidly said, "My name is Libby."

I suddenly realized the words that were spoken over me a few days prior, were preparation for this moment. I was pulling labels off of Libby glasses and this young girl's name was Libby.

I began to prophesy to her. "You have lived most of your life with labels that do not describe you. You are not who you think you are. You are not who people say you are. The Lord is removing the thoughts and concepts that have kept you in bondage. I speak to the false labels that have confused your identity and decree over you that you are delivered from who you think you are and thrust into who God says you are. From this day forward, the Lord is giving you a new identity as His daughter. You are royalty! Rise up and realize the false labels are gone and your new identity is released to you."

She was visibly moved by the prophecy. After the service, I was able to visit with her and give her a deeper understanding of false identity versus true identity. Knowing who you are according to the Word of God removes false identities and makes it possible for you to become a friend of the Lord. God called Abraham His friend. Jesus spoke these words in John:

> *I no longer call you servants, because a servant does not know his master's business. Instead, I have called you friends, for everything that I learned from my Father I have made known to you.*
>
> John 15:15

Elisha's servant did not have the ability to see in the realm of the Spirit until Elisha prayed for his eyes to be opened. When the eyes of his heart were opened, he too could see the armies of the Lord surrounding them, protecting them from the army of man.

Identity is key to recognizing, receiving, and operating in the seer gift. I am not a sinner, saved by grace. I have a new identity: I am a daughter of the King of kings and the Lord of lords. Yes, I am also a friend of God. I want to know His thoughts; I want to know His mind. I often tell people that I have lost my mind; I have traded it in for the mind of Christ. In reality, I want to know the Lord, as one would know a friend as Abraham did. We have the promise that we can have His thoughts within us.

I love having coffee with a friend, sitting down at a comfortable table, sharing our thoughts, hopes and dreams with each other. I think it's my love language—meaningful conversation. So when the Lord shares His thoughts with me—His heart about a situation, His dreams for my family, His dreams for the nations of the earth—I want to listen. I desire to have a listening heart, one that not only shares my thoughts but is also open to hear the thoughts of others and the thoughts of the Spirit of God.

I believe that relationship is cultivated similar to cultivating a friendship with a longtime friend. There is trust that builds in any relationship until proven otherwise by betrayal, gossip, accusation, or façade. We all know that God can be trusted, yet we see Him through fallen eyes, eyes that have seen pain, disappointment, rejection, and fractured dreams. I want to see Him as He really is, one who can be trusted, one who can lead me beside quiet waters or through the valley of death. It doesn't matter where He leads me, I must follow. He has not betrayed me; He has not disappointed me. I have set myself up to be disappointed by my own delusions, but that is not God's fault. I have learned that He is right and where we disagree, I am in the wrong. My perceptions of who He is are continually changing as I allow His Spirit to reveal Him to me. Until that happens, I have little hope of demonstrating who He is to others. I can tell you what the Word says about Him. I can read you verses from the Bible about what He did on the earth. I can tell you historically who men say He is or was, but if I really want to know Him, I must seek Him and allow His Spirit to reveal Him to me and through me.

There is an old song.... I know, I know! I keep bringing them up, but many of them have impacted my life at a crucial time in it. The Holy Spirit brings them up periodically to remind me of our times of crossing over from what I thought I knew into true revelation of my Father God. So here it is:

TO KNOW HIM ALONE

To know Him, to know Him is the cry of my heart.
Spirit reveal Him to me.
To hear what He's saying brings life to my soul.
To know Him, to know Him alone.
To know You, to know You is the cry of my heart.
Jesus, Your face now I seek.
To hear what You're saying brings life to my soul.
To know You, to know You alone.

*****

But the natural (unbelieving) man does not accept the things (the teachings and revelations) of the Spirit of God, for they are foolishness (absurd and illogical) to him, and he is incapable of understanding them, because they are spiritually discerned and appreciated. (and he is unqualified to judge spiritual matters). But the spiritual man (the spiritually mature Christian) judges all things (questions, examines and applies what the Holy Spirit reveals), yet is himself judged by no one (the unbeliever cannot judge and understand the believer's spiritual nature). For who has known the mind and purposes of the Lord, so as to instruct Him? But we have the mind of Christ (to be guided by His thoughts and purposes).

I Corinthians 2:14-16 AMP

So, let's finish up our journey into receiving and activating the seer realm.

PERCEIVE

Jesus is speaking to His disciples in Matthew 13 about gifts within them that they had not yet fully activated. His disciples opened up the conversation with this question: "Why do you speak to the people in parables?"

He proceeds to tell them of an ability they did not know they had. He invited them into a realm they had briefly accessed.

He replied, "Because the knowledge of the secrets of the kingdom of heaven has been given to you, but not to them. Whoever has will be given more, and they will have an abundance. Whoever does not have, even what they have will be taken from them. This is why I speak to them in parables:

"Though seeing, they do not see;
though hearing, they do not hear or understand.
In them is fulfilled the prophecy of Isaiah:
"'You will be ever hearing but never understanding;
you will be ever seeing but never perceiving.
For this people's heart has become calloused;
they hardly hear with their ears,
and they have closed their eyes.
Otherwise they might see with their eyes,
hear with their ears,
understand with their hearts
and turn, and I would heal them.'

> *But blessed are your eyes because they see, and your ears because they hear. For truly I tell you, many prophets and righteous people longed to see what you see but did not see it, and to hear what you hear but did not hear it.*
>
> Matthew 13:11-17

We too are disciples of Jesus. I believe this declaration from Jesus of spiritual sight belongs to us. The Word is alive and full of power. Our eyes are blessed because we have the indwelling Spirit of God. I encourage you to pray this scripture for yourself.

PRAYER OF ACTIVATION

Lord, I receive this declaration of Jesus over His disciples. I too am a disciple of Jesus. I decree the knowledge of the secrets of heaven have been given to me. You have given me spiritual knowledge; I ask you to increase that knowledge by the power of Holy Spirit. I decree my eyes are blessed because they see, and my ears are blessed because they hear.

RECEIVE

Recognize the gift is within you, indicated by daydreams, night visions (dreams), and the ability to picture what isn't there in the natural realm.

When the Lord invited me into spiritual sight, I was afraid to receive it. Unbeknownst to me, I had already received the gift, but had not activated it with acknowledgment of its existence.

Why do we want to perceive and acknowledge this gift? A dream I had caused me and others to pray for my grandson prior to an event that threatened his life. That dream prepared me, equipped me, and caused me to pray prior to enemy attack. My grandson is here today because of the protection of the Lord, the warning in the dream, and the consequent obedience to pray.

ACTIVATE

The seer gift can be turned on and set in motion by Holy Spirit when He is given access to the heart. It becomes more activated with use. When faithfulness is demonstrated, when the seer gift is acted on through obedience to stewarding the visions given, it will grow and open up as a budding flower in the sunshine of God's favor. When we are faithful in little, He will give us much.

Continuing to activate the gift through obedience confirms to the Spirit of God that you will be faithful with what He releases to you. Also, having an awareness that the gift is given through you to benefit others is key to its increase within you.

INTERPRET

Interpreting what we have seen with the eyes of our heart, can be assisted through relationship with other seers. Also, there are tools available that give prophetic interpretation to objects, numbers, and symbols. Asking Holy Spirit for the interpretation of what was seen activates this aspect of the gift. Finding your tribe in the body of Christ also helps with interpretation. Others who operate in this gift can bring impartation, insight, and stewardship to what the Lord has given you. It is important not to be a "Lone Ranger."

So, let's go back to Grandma's garden. She could see what wasn't there yet. I believe we can do the same. What are the dreams in your heart? They are what is not here yet. The Lord puts these dreams within us, showing us purpose, hope, and potential for ourselves and others.

What do we do with those hopes and dreams? We know from scripture that "Hope deferred makes the heart sick, but desire fulfilled is a tree of life" (Proverbs 13:12).

Hope is like the seeds that my grandmother faithfully planted in the soil. She pulled out the weeds that tried to choke out the tender plants. We have to pull the weeds of doubt that keep us from realizing our dreams. So many have allowed the weeds to grow and overpower what they were purposed to bring forth. That's where the seer gift brings light into the situation, recultivating worn-out soil, watering the ground with hope, snapping a photograph of the future and describing it to the receiver. It's in essence saying, "This is where you are going. It's not over until it's over, and it's not over."

The seer sees what God is dreaming of for that person. The seer opens up a realm of light into the darkness of a person's life. It's a beautiful gift. It resides within us, dormant, unopened in many, but laying there as a gift ignored or unseen. My hope is that you will ask the Lord to bring life to the gifts within you, to open your spiritual eyes and ears to see and hear what the Spirit is saying. With His Spirit within you, opportunity awaits.

Please allow the Lord to surround you with those who can help mentor you in the seer gift. I have never been alone in my efforts to see and hear in the Spirit. I have been surrounded by others who have encouraged me, helped me, and mentored me in developing what the Lord has given.

ACTIVATION

Lord,

I want to see what you reveal. I want to activate the gifts within me. I know they are based on your Word, given not for me, but given to help others. Lord, I pray for less of me and more of you to be demonstrated on the earth. Show me who you are so I can reveal you to others. I will not be led by experience alone; I will be grounded in your Word, mentored by others more mature than I. I choose to be teachable as You are cultivating in me the ability to walk in your Spirit. Give me an obedient heart and allow me to always remain humble, knowing the gifts are not from me, but activated through me by your Spirit.

Amen.

About the Author

REGINA SHANK IS THE AUTHOR of *The Standard Bearer - Wisdom From America's Heartland* and *Deliverance To Freedom*. In addition, she has written numerous articles, poems, and devotions for a variety of publications. Her column, *The Standard Bearer*, was published for years by The Carthage Press, Carthage, MO.

She is the founder and President of Missouri Prayer Global Ministries—an apostolic ministry aligned with Network Ekklesia International with Apostle Dutch Sheets, Global Spheres with Chuck Pierce, and Global Transformation International. She is a member of the International Society of Deliverance Ministers. She is also the founder and director of Feeding Inc., a feeding outreach ministry in southwest Missouri.

Regina teaches on prayer, prophetic and strategic intercession, warfare, deliverance, and the importance of a strong personal relationship with Jesus. She has served in several leadership roles in the body of Christ, leading prayer trips to Romania, Italy, Bosnia, Ethiopia, Egypt, Israel, Hungary, Russia, and China. She and her husband, Mick, have three children and five grandchildren.